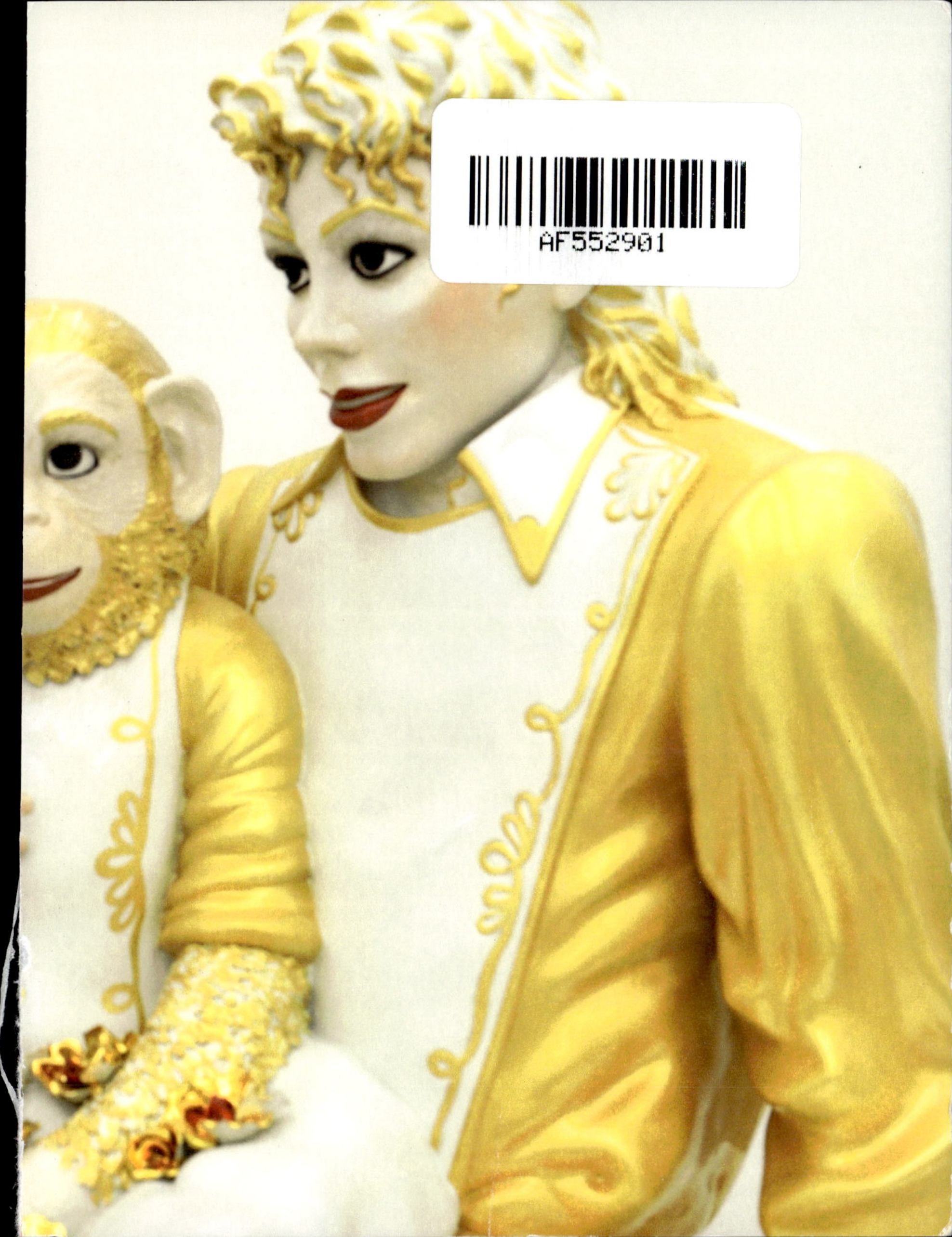
AF552901

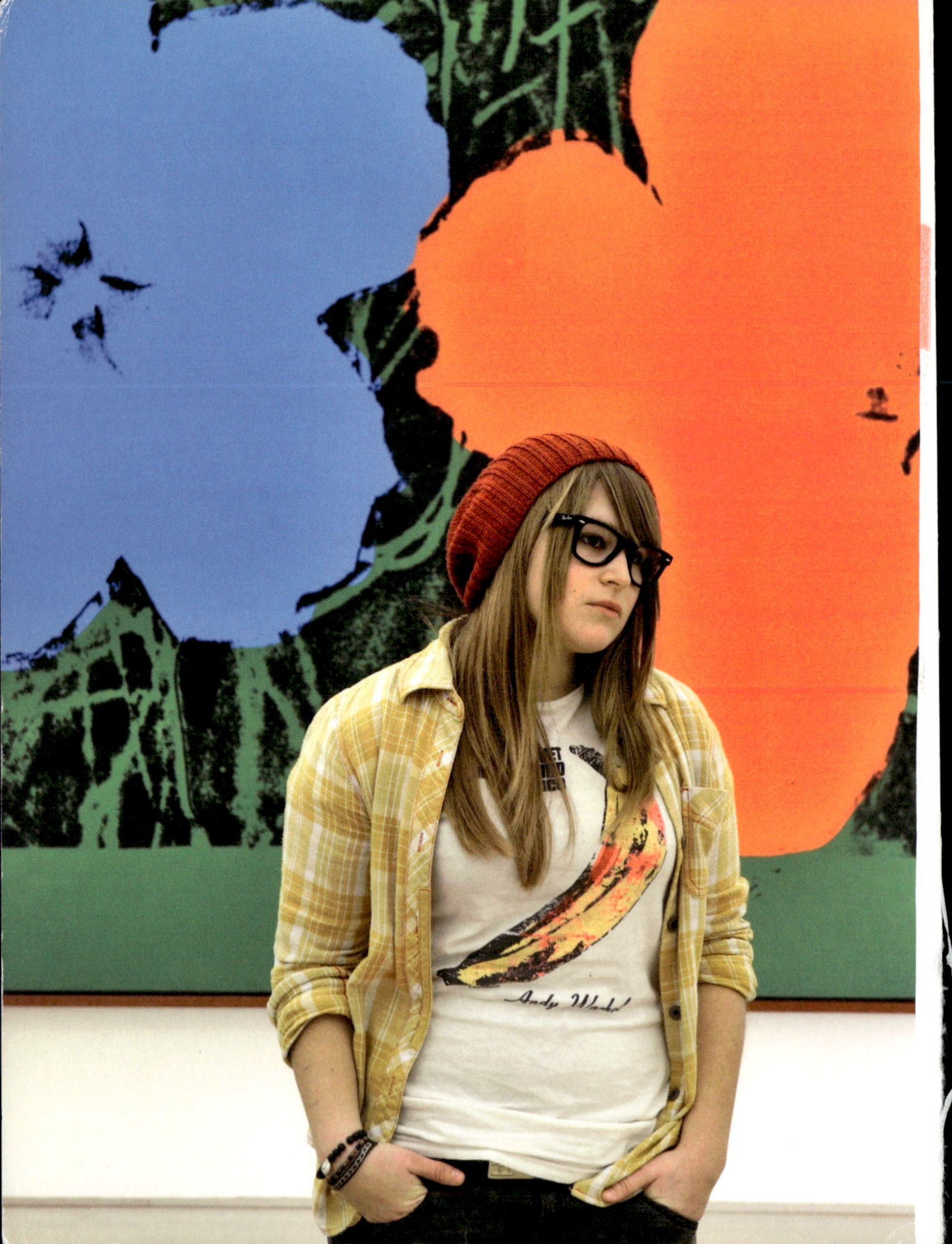
Andy Warhol

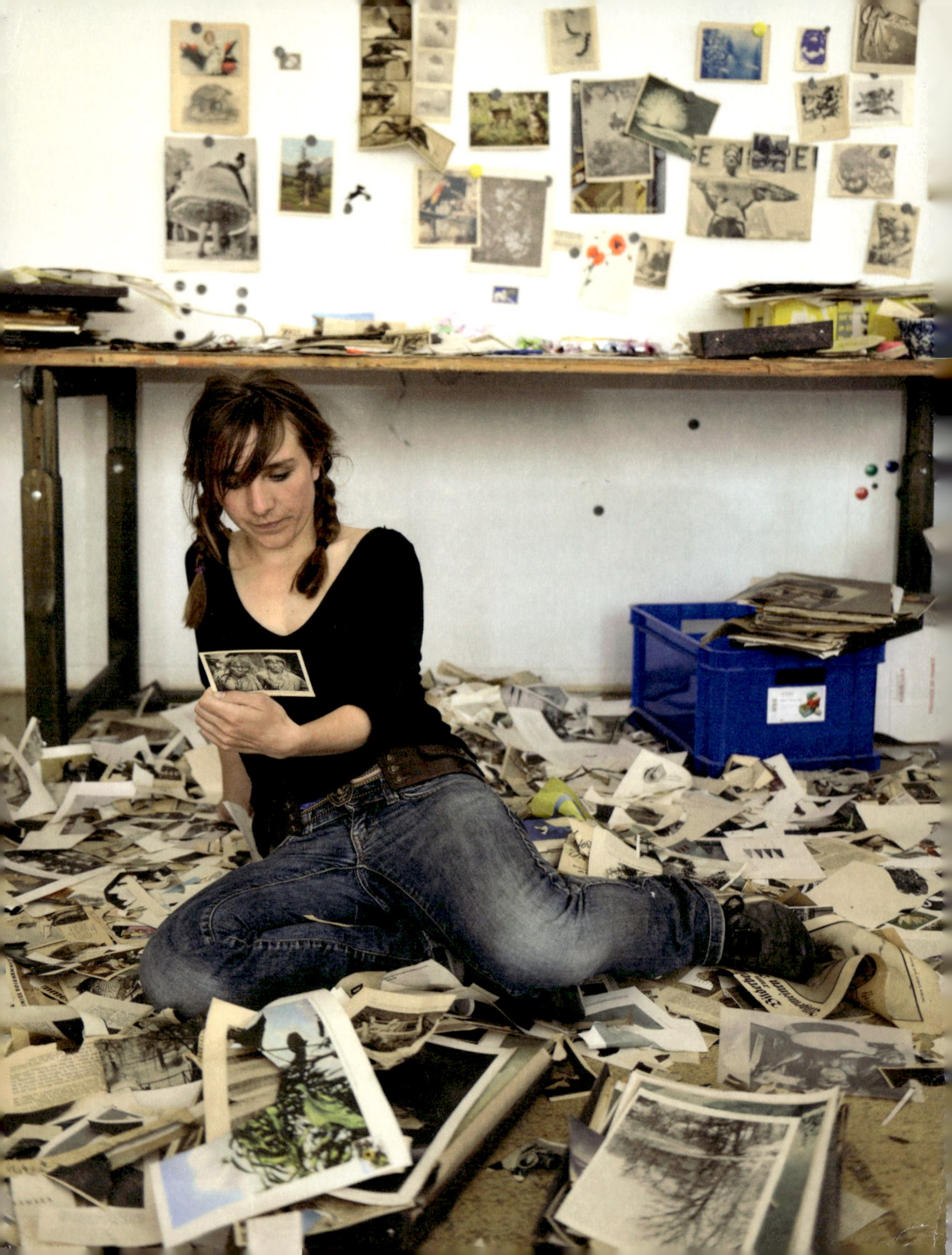

"What is Art?"

Anyone who tries to come to grips with art knows that it opens up new horizons. Art enables us to see the world and ourselves with fresh eyes. But how do we gain access to art? What do we have to know to understand modern and contemporary art? In fact, what *is* art?

This book poses questions and gives answers—in words and pictures. Conceived in close cooperation with young people and specialists, it explains various aspects of art in plain and simple English.

In this volume, the Fondation Beyeler, one of the best-known art museums in Switzerland, has drawn on its many years of experience in art education. As a long-time and committed patron of the arts and sponsor of the Department of Art Education, UBS has made the publication and distribution of this book possible. Together, we hope that our efforts will encourage many, especially young, people to discover art for themselves—and that *What is Art?* is a joy to read!

Sam Keller
Director, Fondation Beyeler

Lukas Gähwiler
CEO, UBS Switzerland

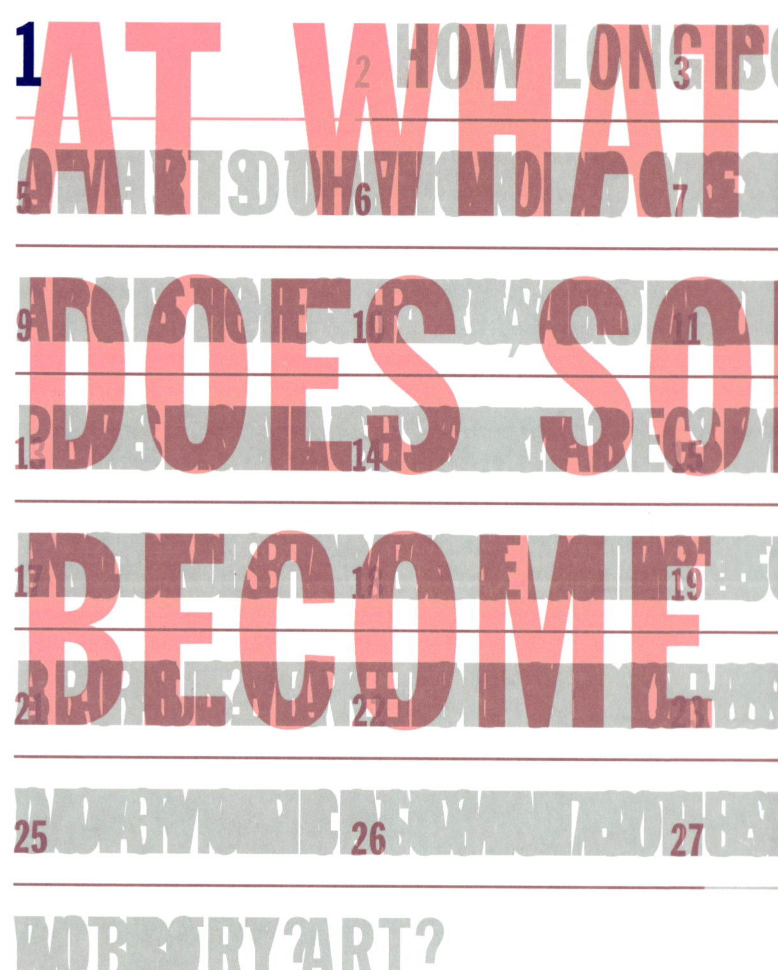
1
AT WHAT
DOES SO
BECOME
2 HOW LONG
3
5
6
7
9
10
11
13
14
15
17
18
19
21
22
23
25
26
27
ART?

POINT
ETHING
RT?

1 AT WHAT POINT DOES SOMETHING BECOME ART?

There is no authority capable of determining once and for all what art is. No one can provide binding guidelines or definitions. The only thing we can be sure of is that art has to do with appreciation. Works of art are praised, loved, or harshly criticized. "This isn't art!" declare some, while others reply, "This is a groundbreaking, major work!"

Where does art begin, and where does it end? Let's look at this question from three angles:

The work of art — Does the material in which it is executed determine whether a work is art or not? In the past, this was in fact the case. An artwork had to be made out of certain materials, such as oil paint, marble, or bronze. Nowadays, we are also confronted with ordinary materials like wire or rubber. Some works are made of platinum and diamonds, such as Damien Hirst's* skull (*For the Love of God*), while others consist of simple snippets of paper, like Kurt Schwitters's collages.

Does art lie in the manner in which a thing is made? The huge paper cutouts of the American artist Kara Walker demonstrate excellent crafts skills. Other artists don't even work on their objects. Marcel Duchamp just chose an article of mass

* For the life dates of the artists mentioned in this book, see the index of artists' names on page 204.

production, such as a bottlerack, and put it in a museum. The elaborately carved and painted wood sculptures of the American artist Jeff Koons are very impressive—yet, the artist didn't create them with his own hands, but had them made by skilled carvers in Oberammergau, Germany, based on his specifications.

In the twentieth and twenty-first centuries, it is not uncommon to see the material of a work of art virtually evaporate. Sometimes, a line of type remains, as with Jenny Holzer, or a little heap of pollen, as with Wolfgang Laib. In such cases, the artistic effort lies in developing a brilliant idea. In other words, we can't define works of art on the basis of their material or the way it's used. So let's look at the people who make art—the artists.

The artists — From the artist's point of view, the question "At what point does something become art?" is as fundamental as it is familiar. And it leads to many other questions: What is art and what should it do? What effects can it have? Is what I make good enough? Have I been able to put my ideas into practice? Have I selected the right materials for the task? Is the work finished? Will other people understand it correctly? Artists can create the most diverse works of art, but whether they are recognized, accepted, appreciated, valued, and bought as art is beyond their control.

The public — In the end, it's other people or the public who decide what art is and what not. Something becomes art because it's recognized as such. First of all, in the context of the art world: works must be shown in exhibitions, discussed in art publications, and bought by collectors and museums. It can well happen that something is not at first considered to be art, yet later is declared to be. In the twentieth century, for example, it took a long time for photography and film to be regarded as art. And only gradually did works from other cultures, such as those of Africa and Asia, find their way into European galleries and museums. Every age redefines what art is.

Young people sketching Marcel Duchamp's *Bottlerack*, 1961 (cast of the 1914 original), Philadelphia Museum of Art → →→

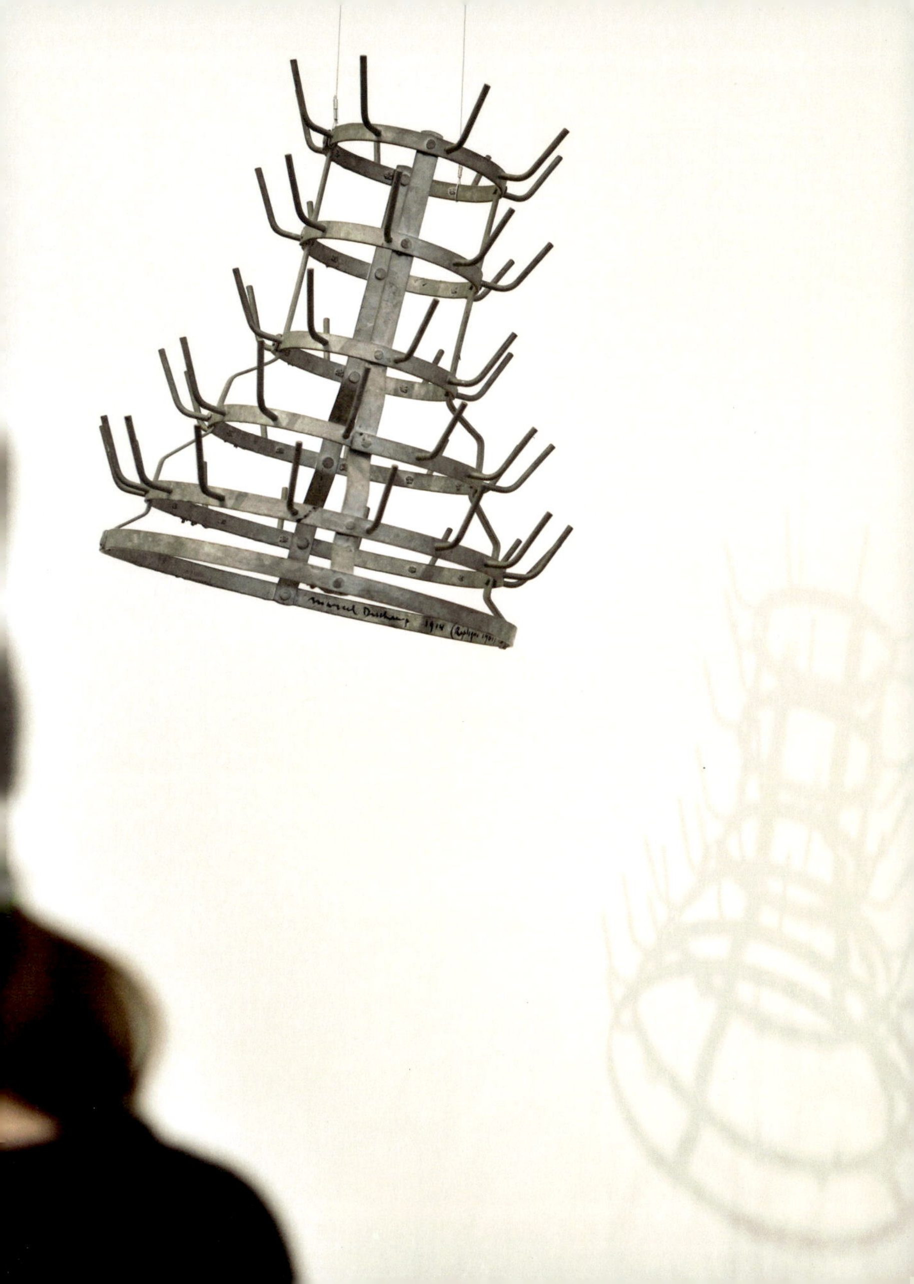
marcel Duchamp 1914

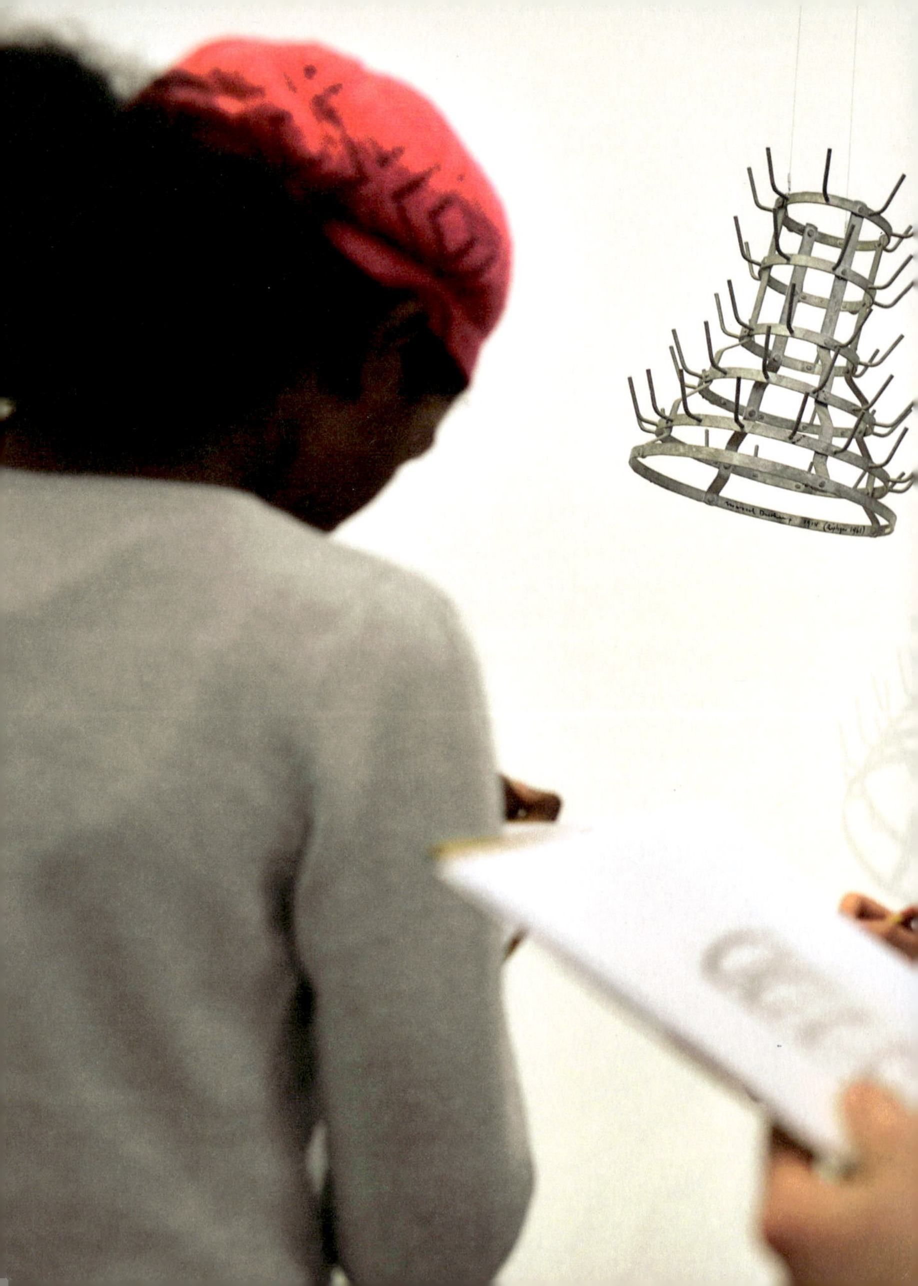

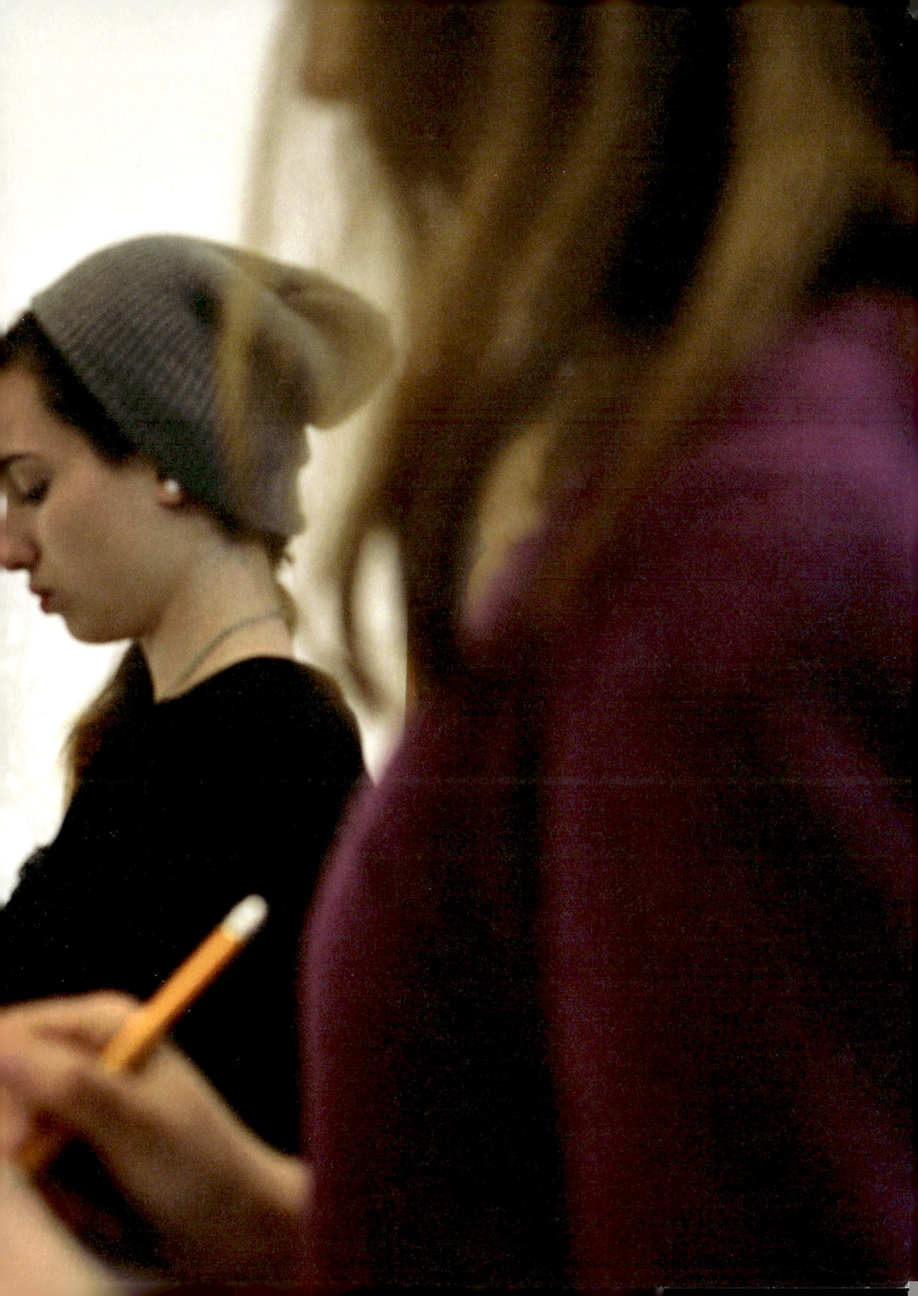

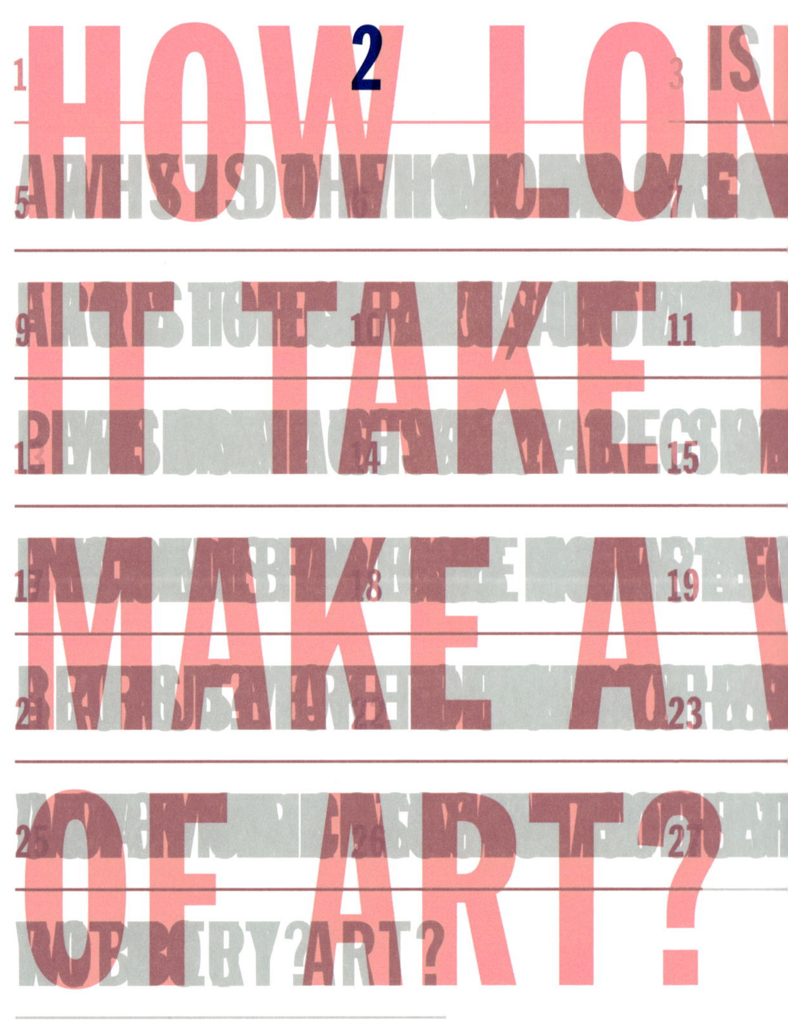

DOES

ORK

2 HOW LONG DOES IT TAKE TO MAKE A WORK OF ART?

The story goes that Claude Monet painted his over-lifesize portrait *Camille* (*Lady in a Green Dress,* 1866) in only four days. Even if we assume that he worked quickly in rough brushstrokes, this is hard to believe.

In the seventeenth century, a Netherlandish painter would sometimes need several months to finish a portrait done with fine brushes and in many layers. In the case of stone sculpture, this would be considered a short period. The Italian sculptor Michelangelo worked on his gigantic marble statue of David for about two and a half years, from autumn 1501 to spring 1504.

A photograph, by comparison, can be taken within a second. Yet, pressing the button is only a small part of the creative process. A photo may be preceded by intensive research and a search for the right motif, or by an elaborate staging, as in the works of Cindy Sherman. And almost always after taking a picture, there follows a phase of selection and manipulation, in the lab or on a computer.

In contemporary art, the creative process is often the subject of a work. The artist On Kawara, for example, began his series of *Date Paintings* on January 4, 1966. Since then, he has painted several thousand small, horizontal-format canvases that show the date of their making, usually on a black background. If he cannot manage to finish a picture in one day, Kawara destroys it.

In performance and video art, the finished work itself has a certain duration and demands that we view it in a very different way. If there were a record for length, Andy Warhol's film *Empire,* showing the Empire State Building in New York in the night of January 25 to 26, 1964, in a single, unmoving shot, must hold it. Here, the passage of time is indicated only by changing light conditions in the sky and the building's illumination. The film lasts eight hours and five minutes.

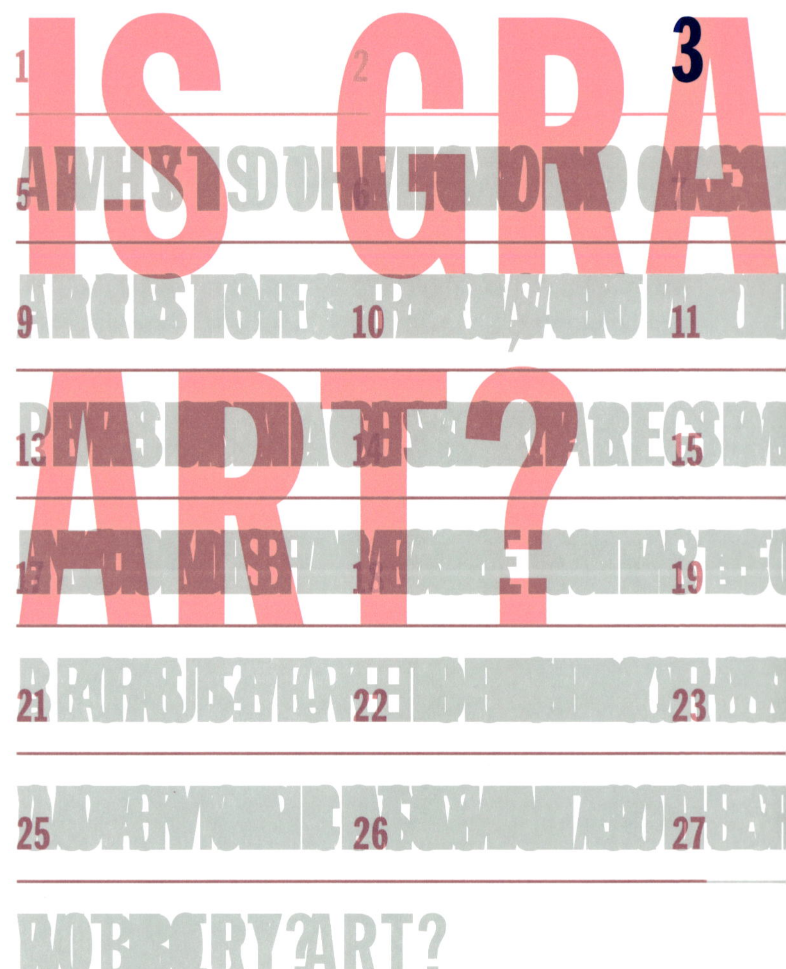
IS GRA
ART?
3

3 IS GRAFFITI ART?

Graffiti is often viewed as vandalism. Unlike conventional painting, not canvas but walls are used as supports. When these walls belong to someone else, applying graffiti to them is illegal.

The results are graphically seen in the case of Harald Naegeli, known as the "Sprayer of Zurich." In the eighties, Naegeli was found guilty of several counts of vandalism and convicted to nine months in prison and was fined about 206,000 Swiss francs. While attempting to escape, he was arrested in Germany, where he was sent back to Switzerland, despite the protests of the artist Joseph Beuys and the former German Chancellor Willy Brandt.

Yet, graffiti is also an expression of the human urge to leave lasting impressions on one's environment. The earliest examples are Stone Age cave drawings. Scratched inscriptions and sketches on ancient Roman walls have also survived. Contemporary graffiti emerged in the U.S. in the seventies, when the first "writers" sprayed New York subway cars with their "tags." This rapidly expanded into an entire sprayers' scene with a wide range of individual styles and codes.

Alongside other forms of expression, such as "sticker tagging," "adbusting," and "urban knitting," graffiti today is viewed as art, and labeled Street Art or Urban Art. The former "lawbreaker" Naegeli, too, has since been officially recognized as an artist, with one of his works of graffiti even having been elaborately restored by the Canton of Zurich.

Graffiti began to have an influence on the art scene back in the eighties. At the time, the American artists Keith Haring and Jean-Michel Basquiat earned a fortune from and became world-famous thanks to their graffiti-inspired paintings. In the case of Banksy, on the other hand, we can see how complex the relationship between graffiti and the art market is. When someone chiseled out one of his popular works of rat graffiti from a London wall in 2007 and offered it on eBay, neighborhood resistance caused the auction to be stopped. After all, street art belongs to everybody, doesn't it? That same year, Banksy's work *Bombing Middle England* was sold at a Sotheby's auction for 102,000 pounds. However, instead of being the original graffiti on a house wall in Bristol, it was the same motif sprayed on canvas. But is this still even graffiti?

Young man viewing Nick Walker's *Vandal Girl,* 2012, on Gansevoort Street in New York's Meatpacking District

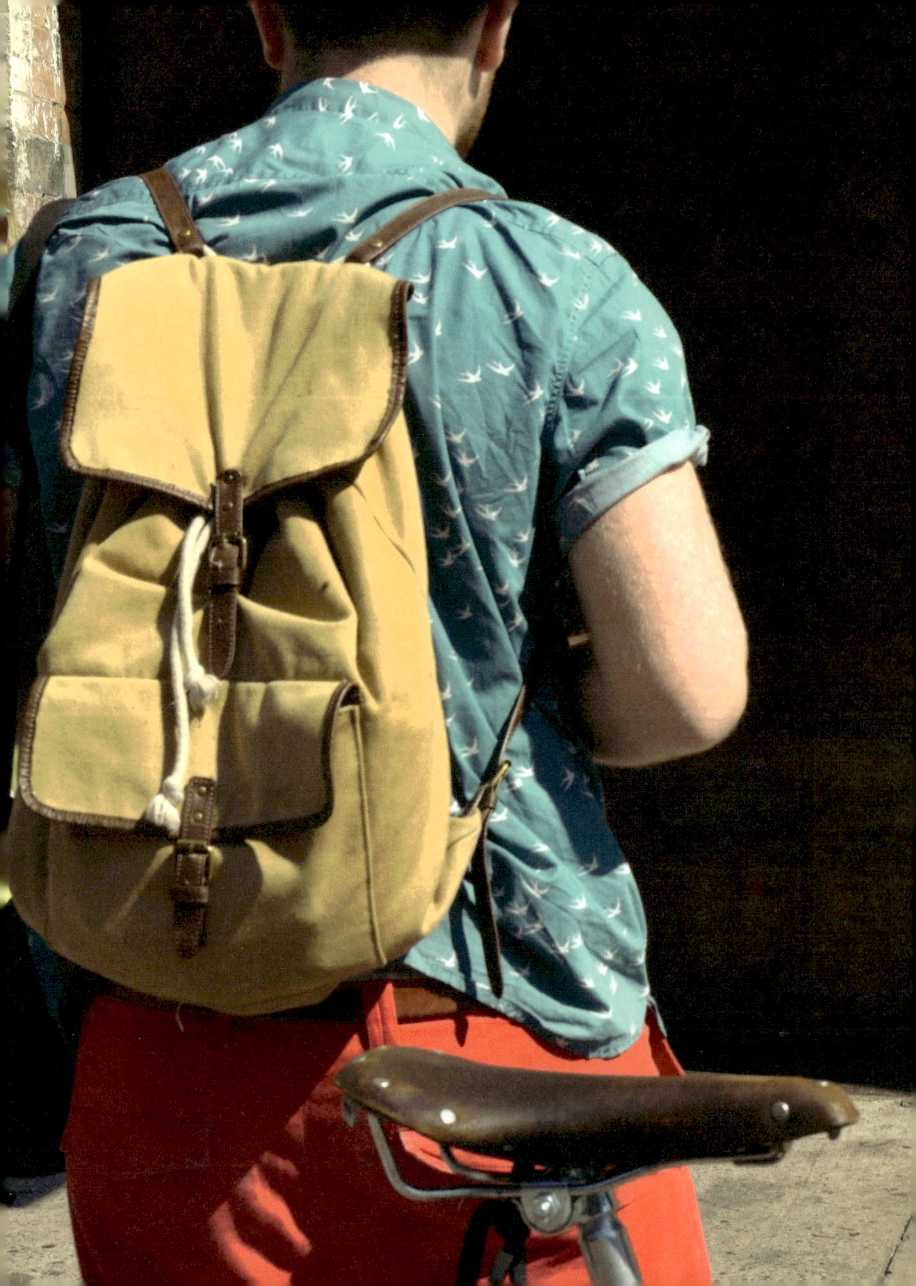

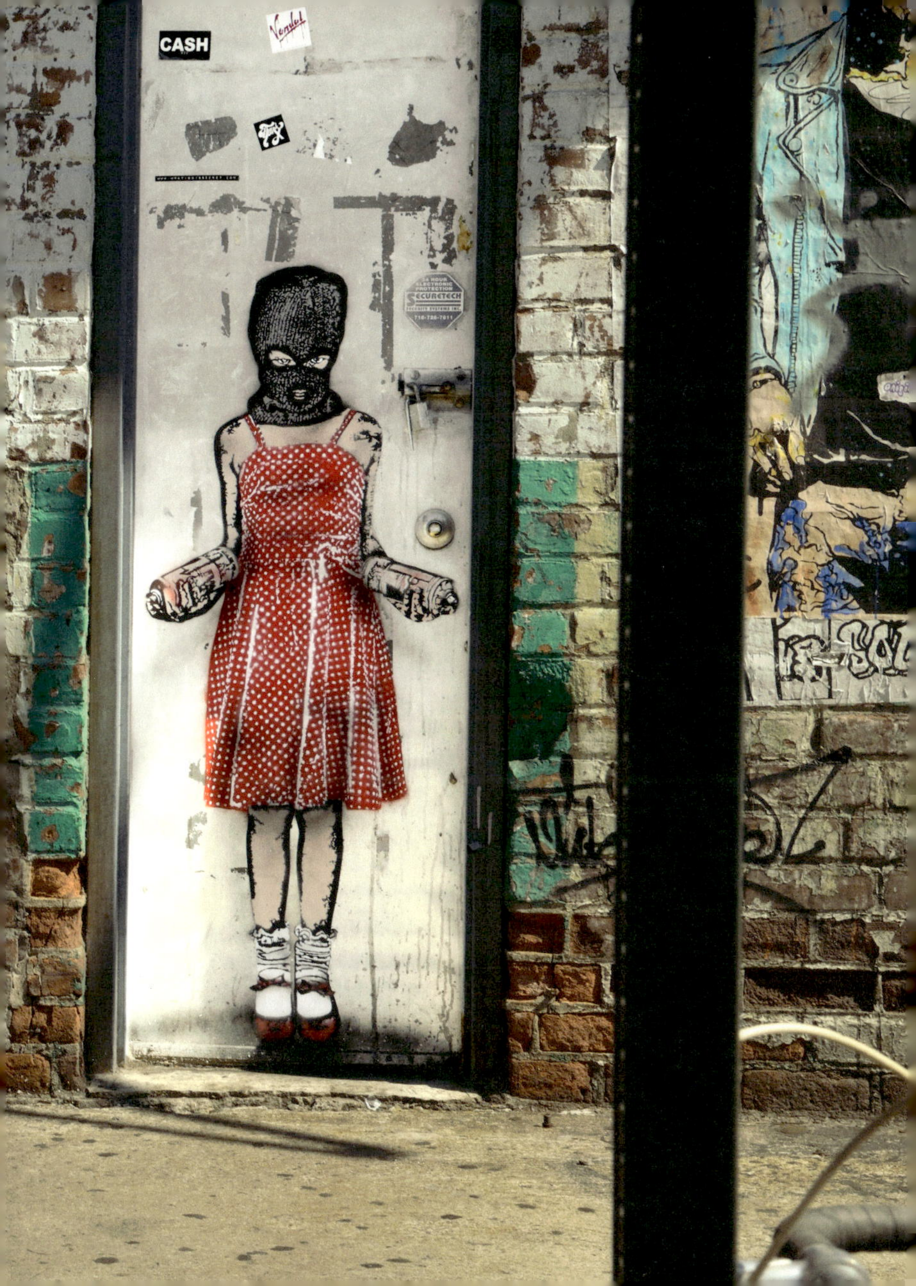
CASH
ELECTRONIC
PROTECTION
SECURETECH

WHAT DOES

ARTIST DO

HE OR SHE

LIKE A WO

1 2 3

5 WHY IS THE 6 HOW 7

9 10 11

13 14 15

17 18 19

21 22 23

25 26 27

ART?

AN
WHEN
DOESN'T
K?

4 WHAT DOES AN ARTIST DO WHEN HE OR SHE DOESN'T LIKE A WORK?

When an artist isn't satisfied with a work, he or she can deal with it in a number of ways: put it aside and wait awhile—maybe it'll look better at some later point in time; keep working on it and altering it until he or she is satisfied; destroy the work and begin a new one.

Continually starting anew and trying out various things is an essential part of the creative process. Many artists don't become clear about their ideas and feelings until they have failed again and again. Whenever something new emerges, change and destruction are always involved. In other words, creation and destruction are only two sides of the same coin, and belong to every phase of the artistic process. The Swiss sculptor Alberto Giacometti, for example, was so persistently plagued by self-doubt that he destroyed his plaster and clay sculptures at night and began all over again the next morning. Many of his pieces survived only because his brother Diego rescued them from the studio, and Alberto decided the next day that they weren't so bad after all.

Visitors taking in the works of Alberto Giacometti and Mark Rothko, Fondation Beyeler, Riehen/Basel → →→

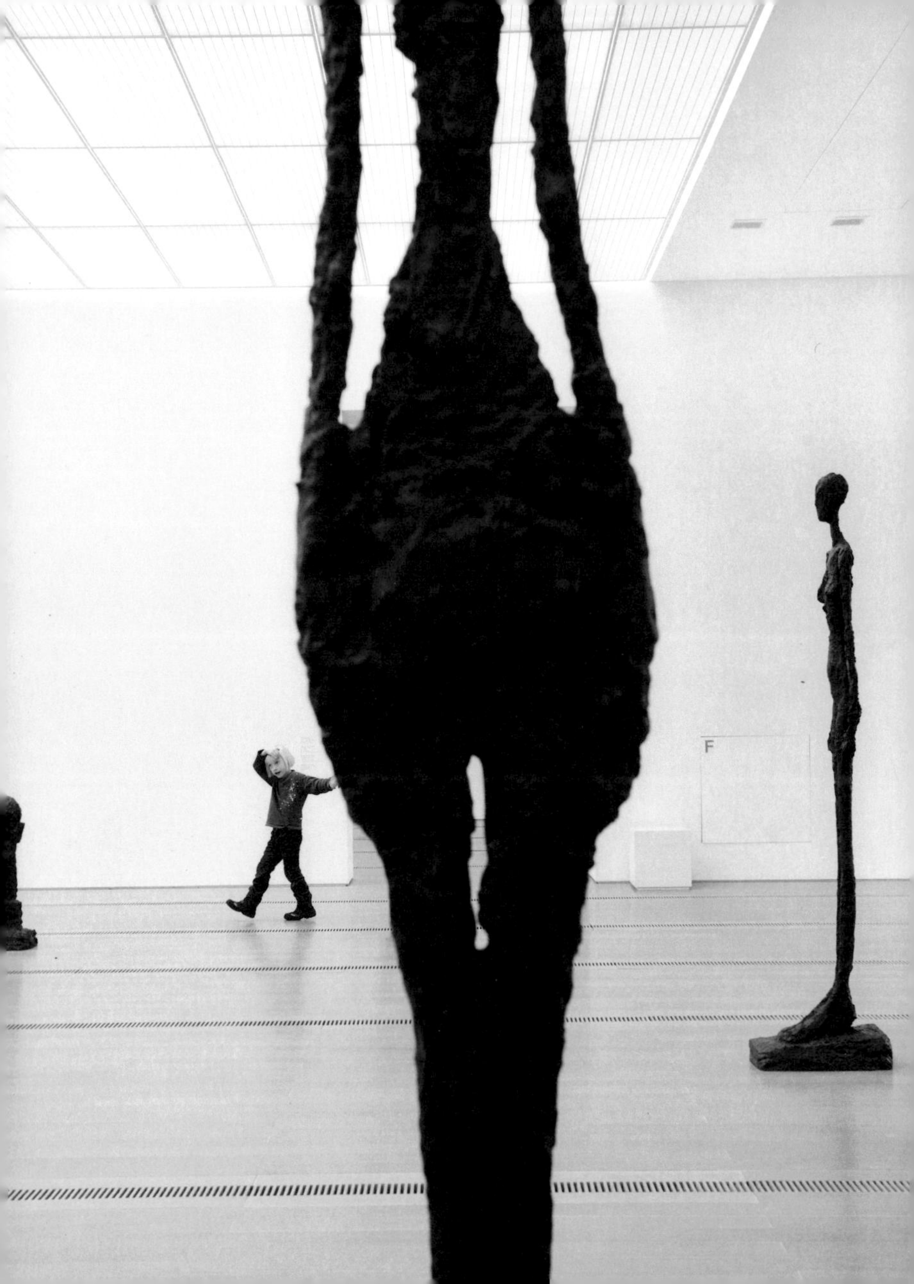
F

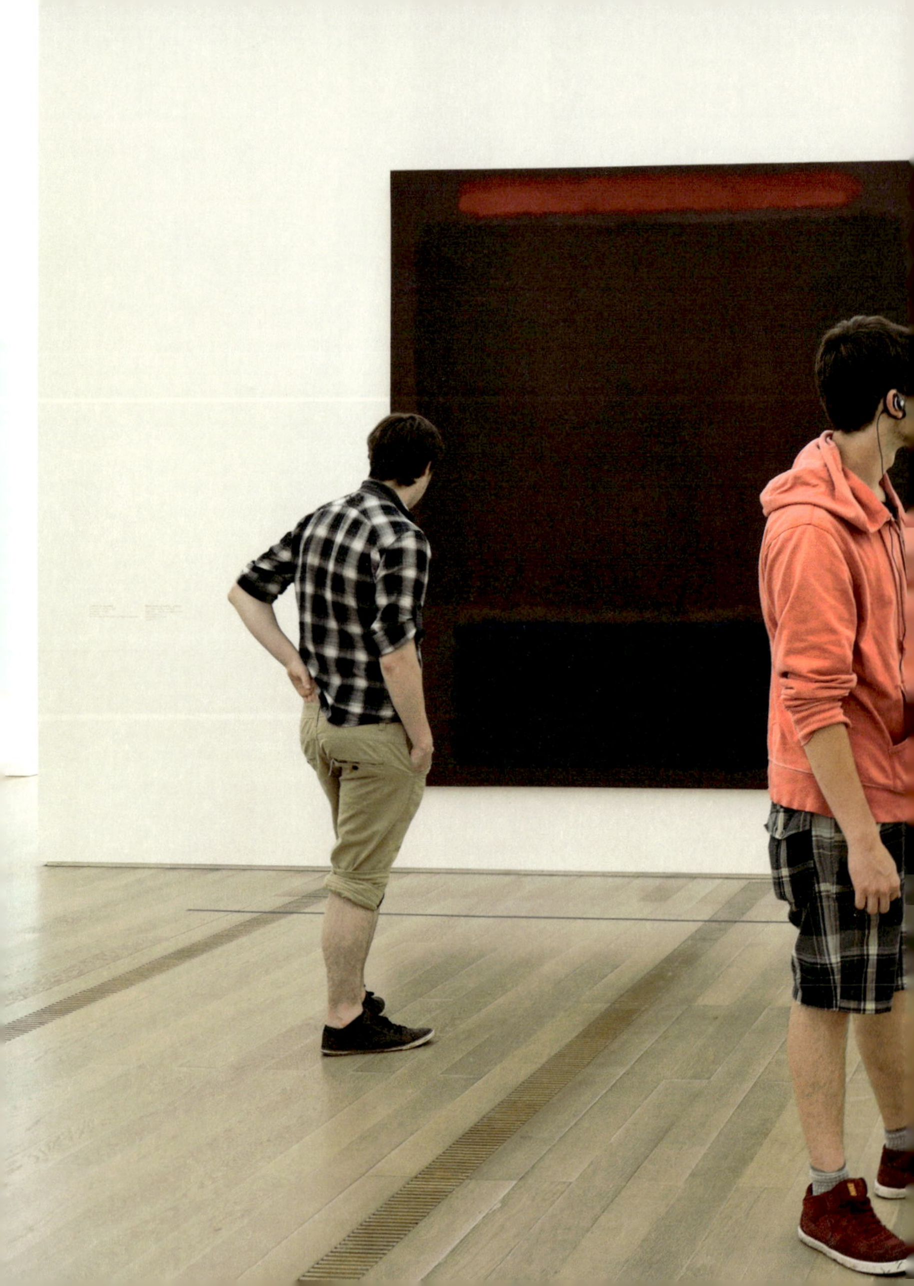

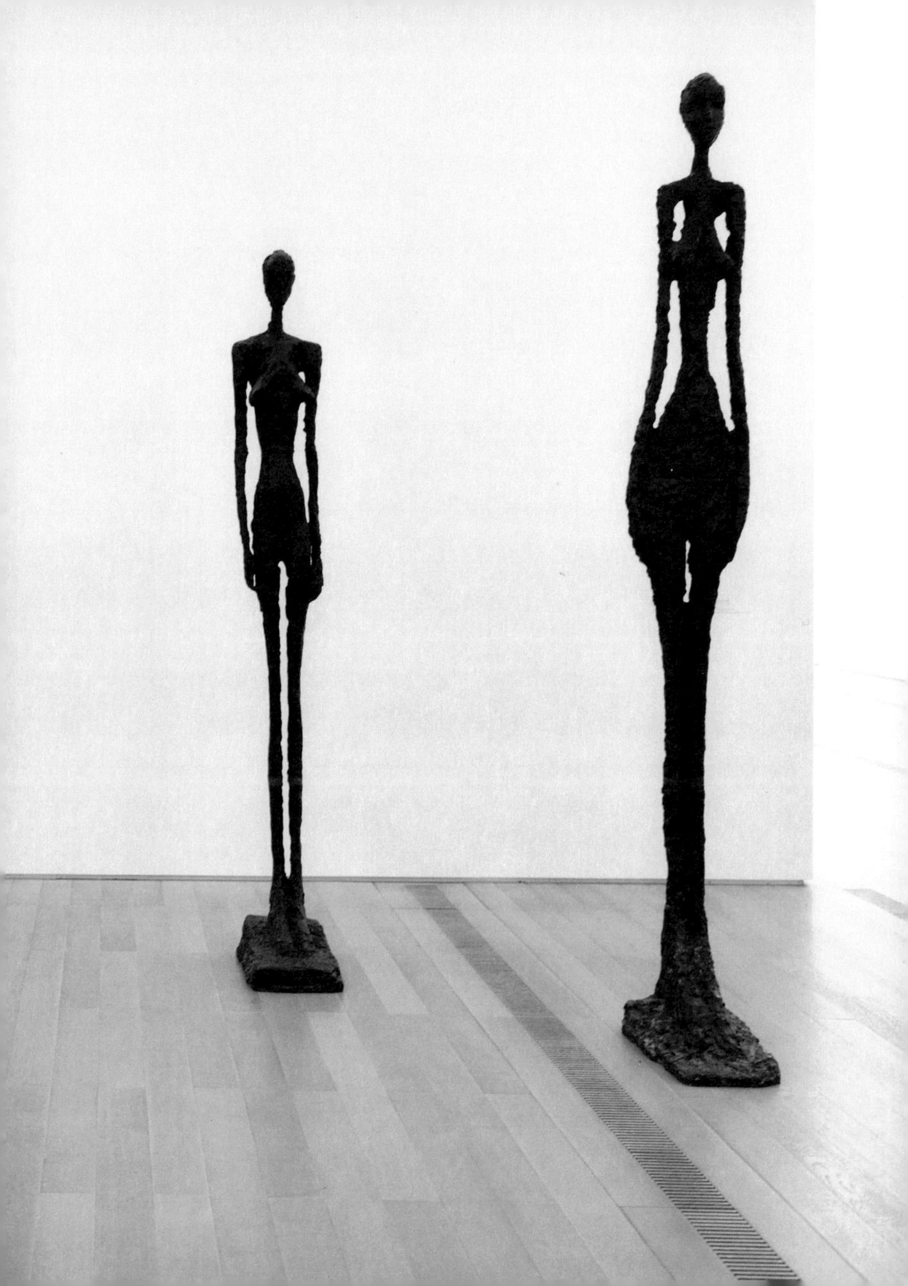

1 2 3

WHY IS

5

6 HOW DO WE A

9 10 11

'MONA

13 14 15

17 18 19

21 22 23

SO FAM

25 26 27

ART?

HE

ISA”

US?

5 WHY IS THE "MONA LISA" SO FAMOUS?

The *Mona Lisa* is considered to be the most famous painting in the world, and is seen by nearly nine million people every year in the Louvre in Paris. Yet, the picture is small, only 77 × 53 centimeters in size.

During his lifetime, the work was not viewed as the most important by the Italian artist Leonardo da Vinci (1452–1519). In 1550, Leonardo's biographer, Giorgio Vasari, was the first to praise the portrait as a good example of the artist's gift of painting something so faithful to nature that it seemed alive. In fact, Leonardo used his famous *sfumato* technique here, to make the eyes and corners of the mouth a bit out of focus, so that the facial expression can't be precisely determined. Then, too, the two halves of the face are slightly asymmetrical, as every face is in real life. In addition, Leonardo placed the horizon to the left and right of the head on a slightly different level. These features cause the viewer's eye to wander back and forth across the image, further increasing the impression of movement and aliveness.

The painting's fame can't be explained solely on the basis of its skilled execution. Many other artworks are excellently made, yet not famous. On the other hand, great numbers of works were extremely popular in the nineteenth century that now merely fill museum depots.

While he was alive, Leonardo da Vinci was known far beyond the borders of Italy, and was even active at the French royal court. Since he painted very few portraits, the *Mona Lisa* had a good chance of becoming famous. Until the French Revolution, however, the painting was in the possession of the royal family, and was not displayed for all to see until the opening of the Louvre on August 10, 1793. In the nineteenth century, romantic art critics described the portrait as the "perfect depiction of mysterious femininity." From that point on, wild speculations began as to the identity of the sitter with the enigmatic smile. Based on Vasari's comments, the woman was long assumed to be Lisa del Giocondo, the wife of a businessman from Florence. This is why the picture is also known as *La Gioconda.* But now, everyone was convinced that Leonardo had portrayed a secret mistress. Additional theories were suggested in the twentieth century. Might the sitter not be Duchess Isabella of Aragon, who, like Leonardo, lived at the Milan court? Or might this even be a portrait of the artist's pupil and supposed lover, Gian Giacomo Caprotti, nicknamed Salaì, made to look like a woman?

The portrait did not become truly world-famous until its spectacular robbery in 1911. For two years, it was believed to be lost forever, until the thief, an artisan who had been employed at the Louvre, tried to sell it to a dealer in Florence. Since then, many artists, including Marcel Duchamp and Andy Warhol, have quoted and commented on the *Mona Lisa* in their own works. Countless reproductions of the picture

have been made, so most people are familiar with it without ever having been to the Louvre. Due to several attacks made on it, the original is now shown behind bullet-proof glass. *Mona Lisa* is guarded like a pop star.

Visitors photographing Leonardo da Vinci's *Mona Lisa,* ca. 1503–06, Musée du Louvre, Paris → →→

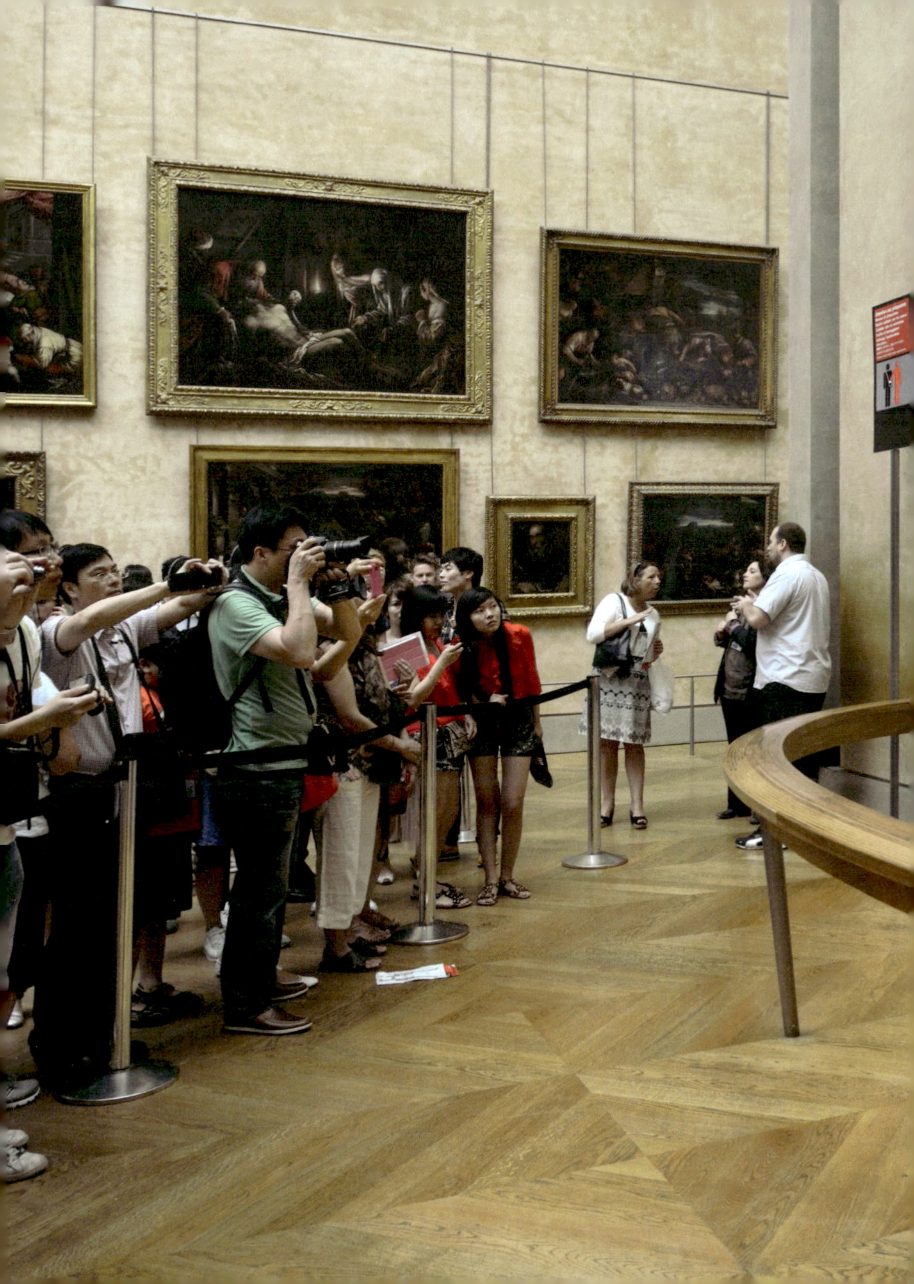

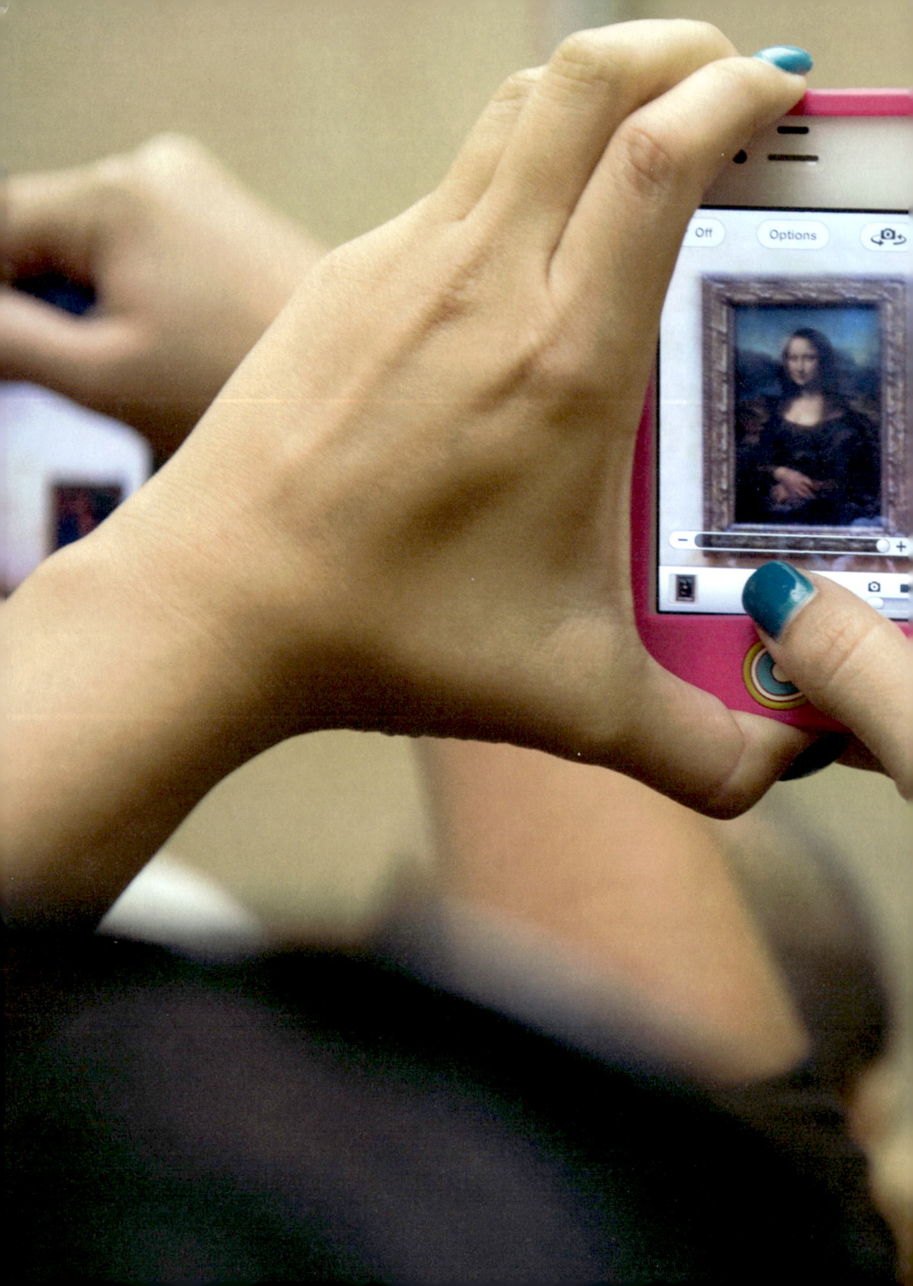
Off
Options

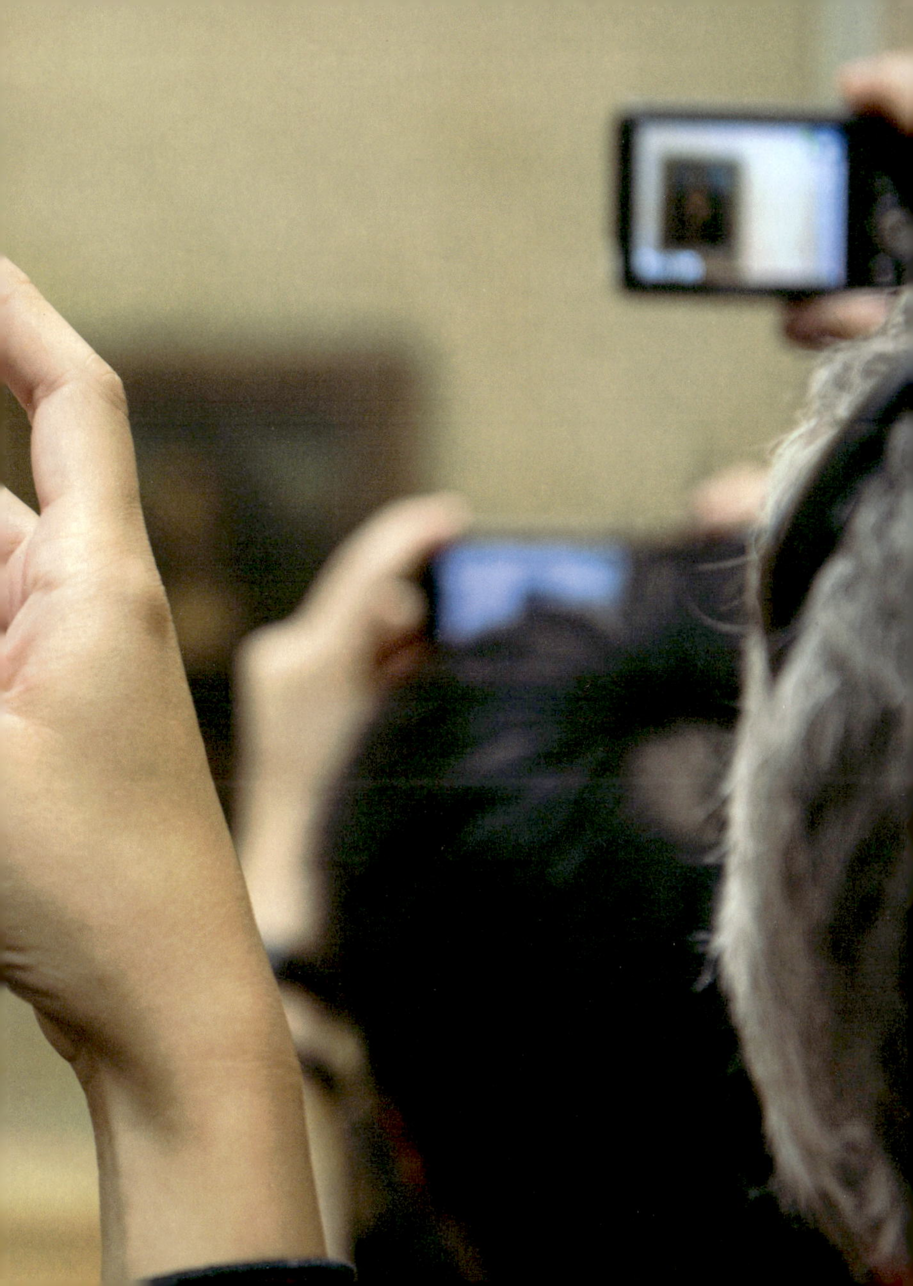

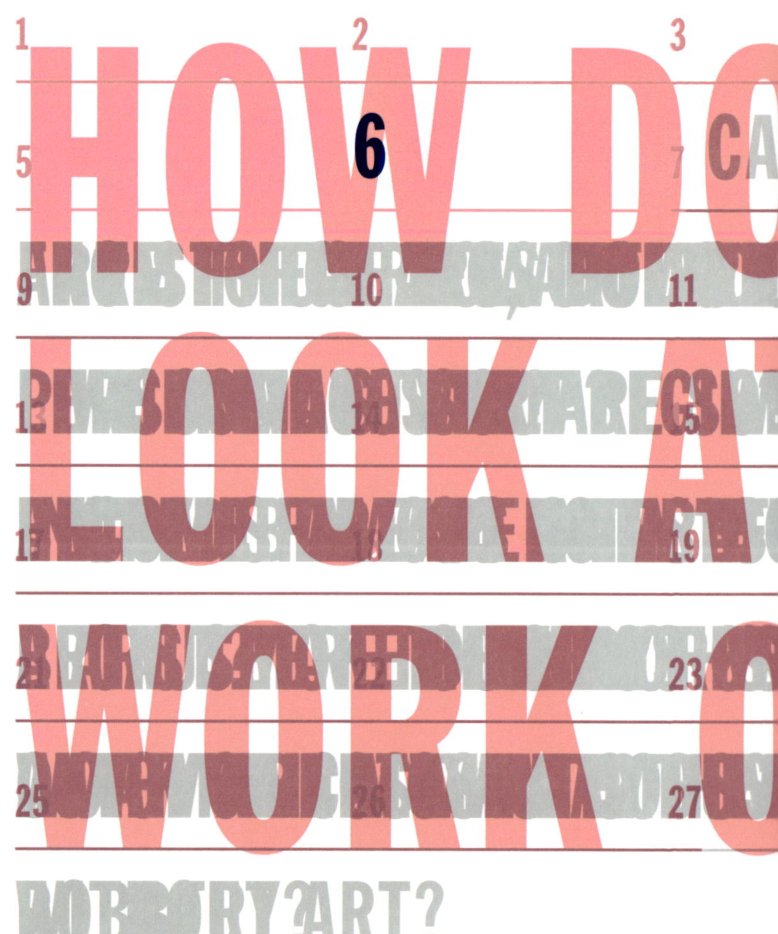

HOW DO
LOOK AT
WORK O

WE A ART?

6 HOW DO WE LOOK AT A WORK OF ART?

According to studies done in museums, the answer is: briefly, very briefly! Museum visitors typically devote only a few seconds, or fractions of a second, to each work of art. Walking through the exhibition rooms, their gaze rarely remains fixed for any length of time. One might conclude that it's the eye that decides what's worth looking at and what not. Since museums often contain hundreds of pictures, this fleeting "survey" is hardly surprising. What is surprising is that we nevertheless sometimes become deeply absorbed in works of art. Sometimes, we are suddenly moved by a painting or sculpture. We are confronted by a color combination, a mysterious pictorial subject, or a striking material or format. Often, we don't even realize what there is to see in the work, but remain standing in front of it anyway, wondering what it's all about.

Some works immediately overwhelm us, while others may take years to sink in. Sometimes, it's love (or horror!) at first sight, sometimes, a gradual awakening. At first, we often see only things we already know and are familiar with. We walk through a museum not only with our eyes open but also carrying a "virtual rucksack." This contains our thoughts, expectations, prejudices, and feelings. We look at a work of art first of all from our own standpoint, and only gradually begin to realize that it has a standpoint of its own. It challenges us, and begins to "look back" at *us.*

An involvement with art is so interesting because it leads to a kind of dialogue, a mutual getting-to-know each other. The contents of our "rucksack" get all mixed up, maybe even repacked, and sometimes we are so carried away by a work of art that we can't help returning to look at it again and again. It may even stick in our mind for years and years, and—strange as it may sound—become part of our life.

Two children in front of Jeff Koons's sculpture *Naked,* 1988,
Fondation Beyeler, Riehen/Basel

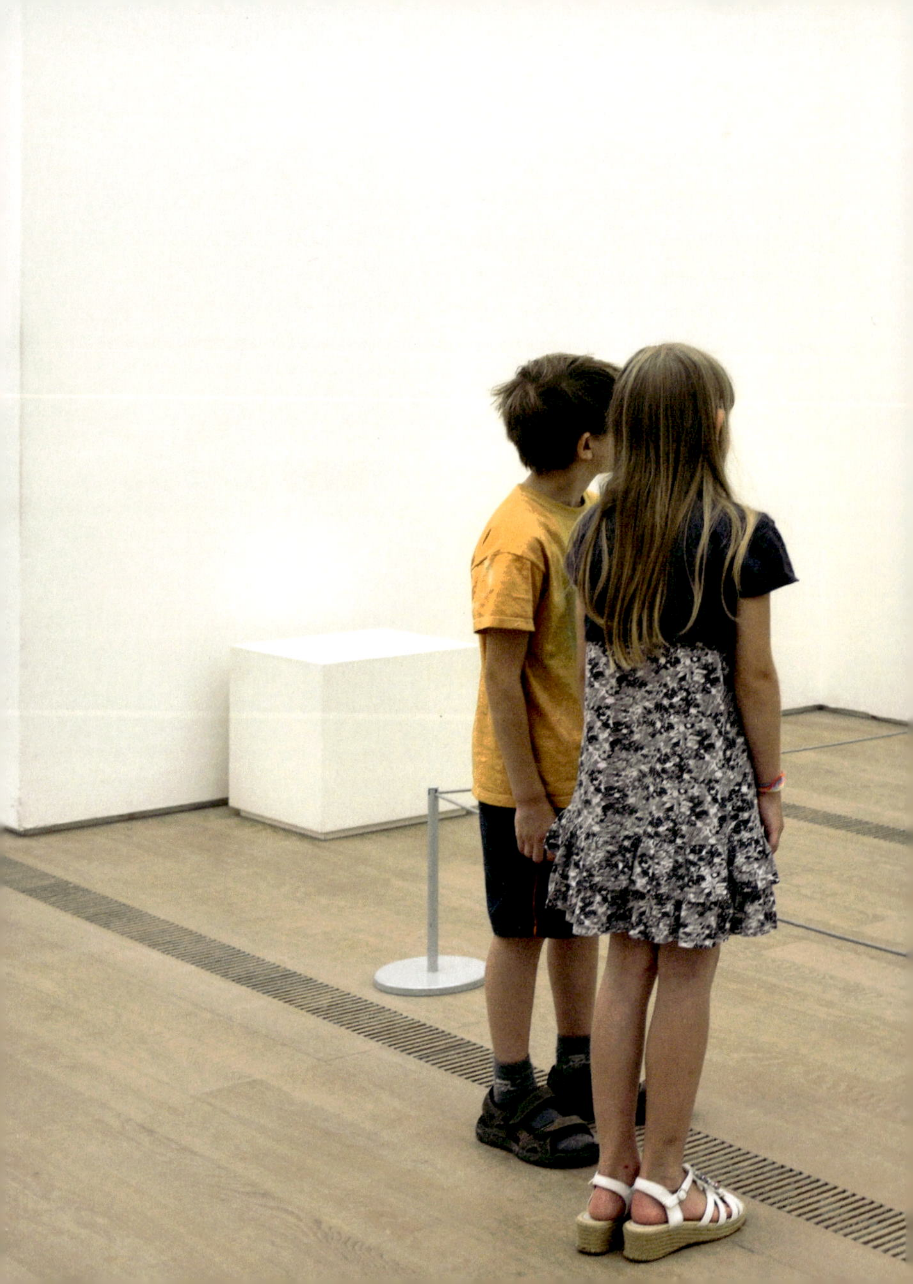

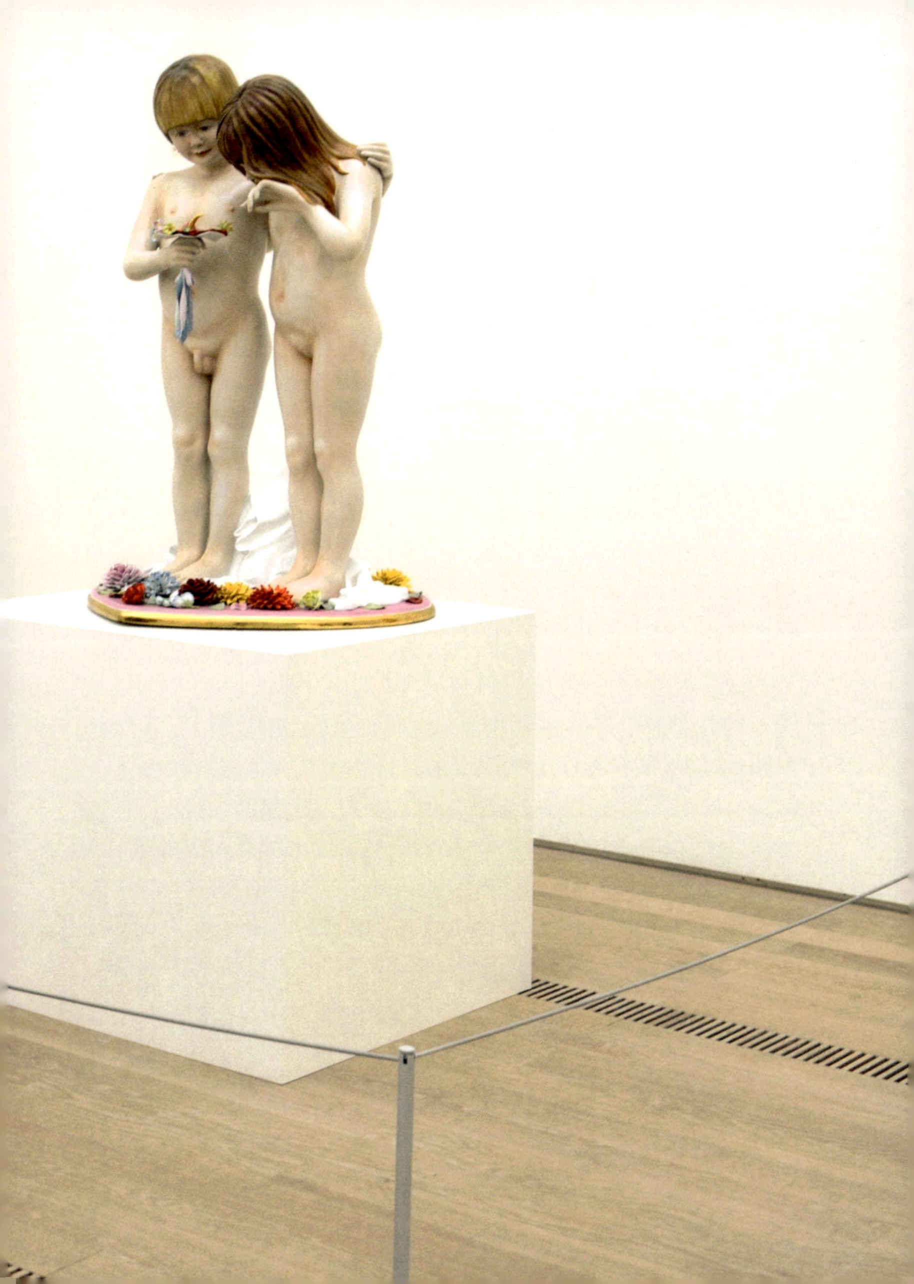

What is art?

“With art, I make what is invisible in me visible. For me, art defines beauty, because beauty always lies in the eye of the viewer.”

Leah Borer

“Art is everything that makes a personal impression on you. It’s what robs from some a short, and from others a longer, moment of their time and triggers emotions in every respect.”

Lucie Fürst

“Art is a colorful blot of paint consisting of a wild mixture of visualized feelings.”

Gina Labhart

“Art is (not) ART(y), a way of expressing yourself. — Art is a language that has no rules, but is (not) understood anyway. — Anybody can paint, but painting is not a liberating process for everybody. — Anything becomes art when it is your own: your own in its essence, unique, and when it contains the artist’s innermost feelings.”

Salome Jermann

“Art is everything and nothing, it’s individual, it’s free of rules, because art is imagination and excitement. Art is everything you understand it to be, and it’s full of emotions and stories.”
Miriam Kuoni

“That an artist succeeds in perceiving and representing in his own way the ‘I,’ with head and hand, heart and mind. That, for me, is art.”
Philomina Chakkalakkal

Students majoring in Visual Arts, Laufental-Thierstein High School, Laufen

Leah Borer, Lucie Fürst, Gina Labhart, Salome Jermann, Miriam Kuoni, and Philomina Chakkalakkal (from back to front) in Richard Serra’s sculpture *Intersection,* 1992, on Theaterplatz in Basel

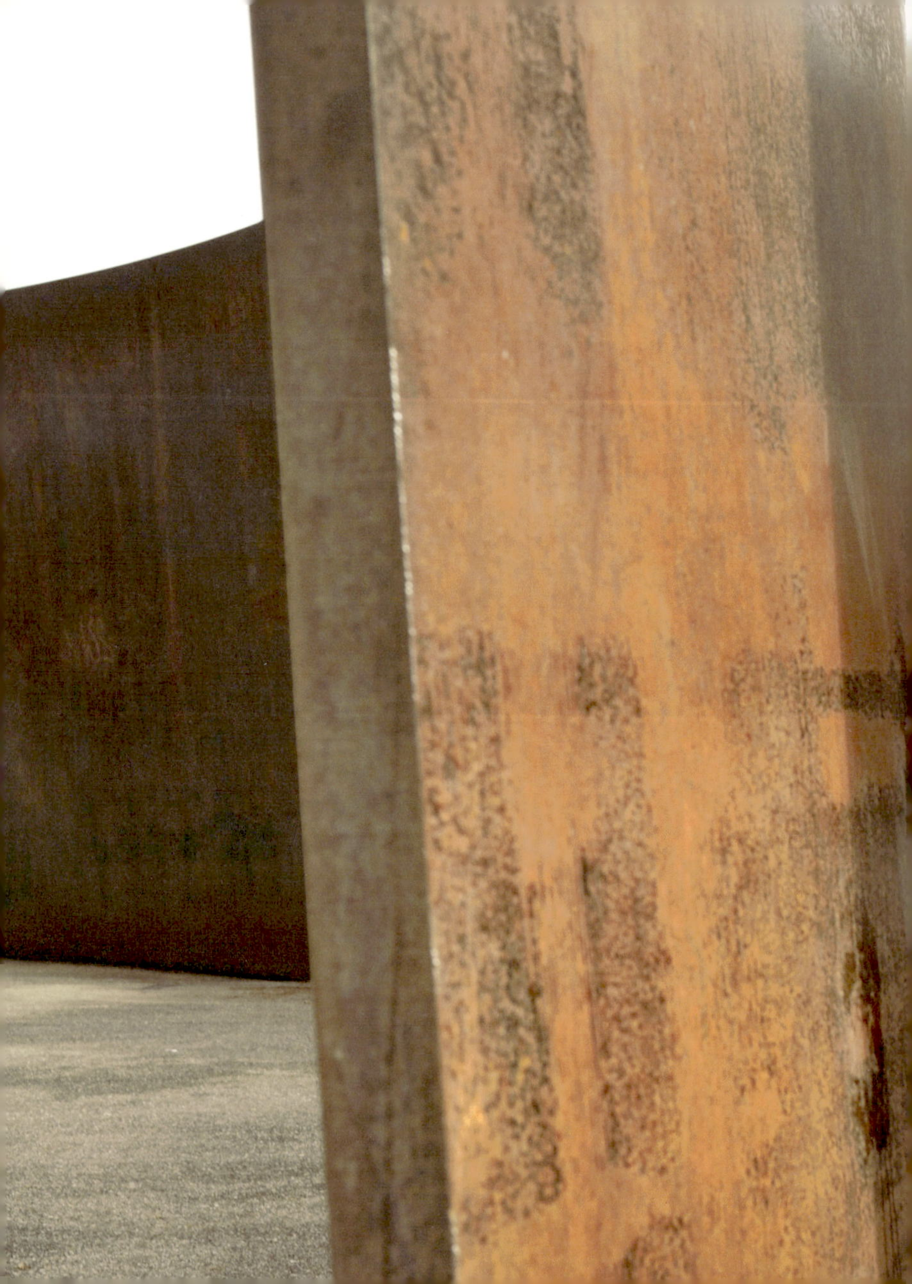

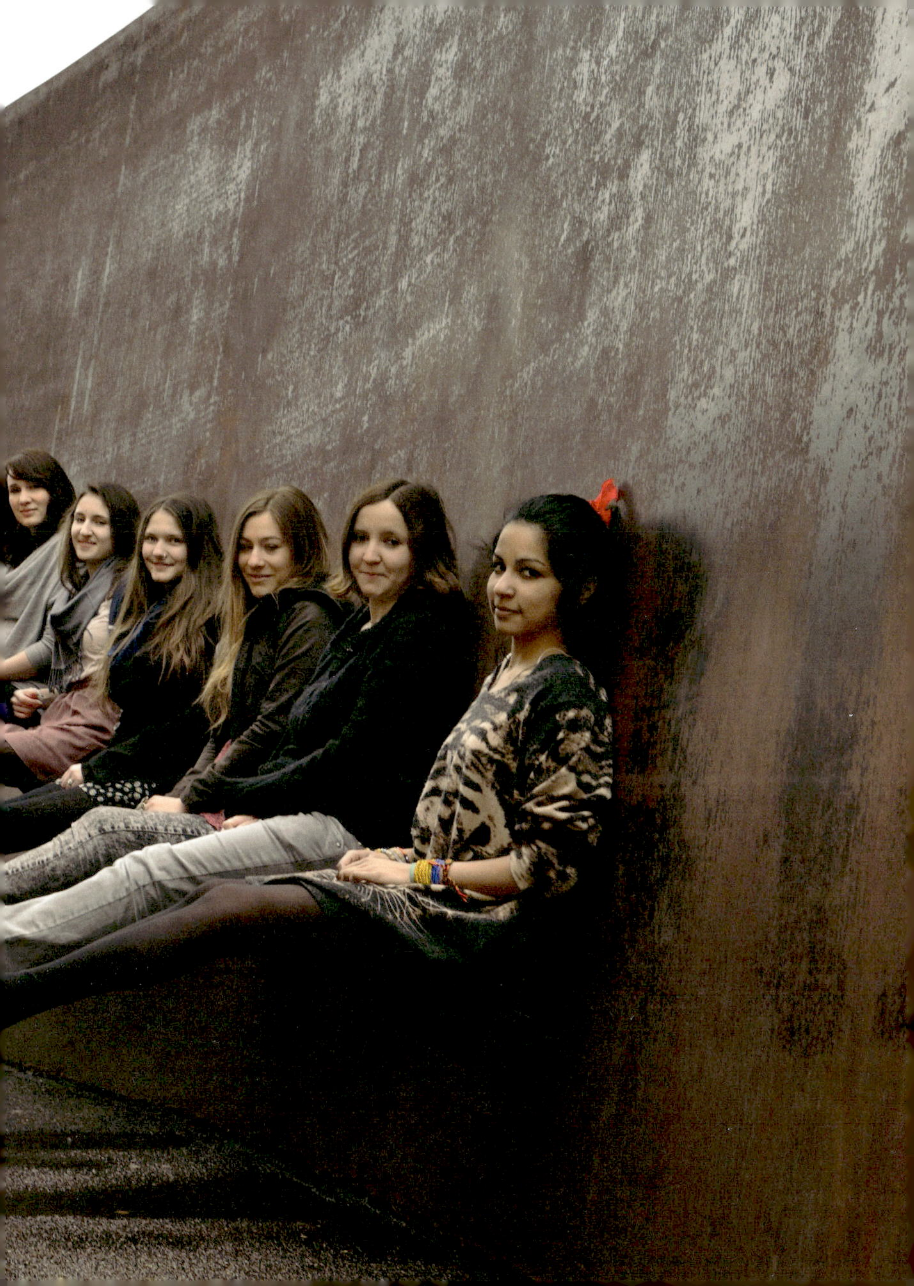

CAN ARTIS
LIVING FRO
ART, OR DO
A SECOND

7

ART?

S MAKE A

THEIR

THEY HAVE

OB?

7 CAN ARTISTS MAKE A LIVING FROM THEIR ART, OR DO THEY HAVE A SECOND JOB?

The idea of the "free artist" who lives solely from selling his or her art is a fairly recent one. For centuries, artists worked for the Church or rich cities, or lived at aristocratic courts, which they decorated with their artworks. As a result, they were well-off, but at the expense of being artistically dependent on the interests and tastes of their supporters, or "patrons."

It was not until the rise of the moneyed middle class in the northern Netherlands in the sixteenth century that an art market developed, in which painters like Rembrandt and Jan Vermeer vied for customers. Still, a large number of these "free artists" were unable to survive without occasional commissions or rich patrons. Those who worked independently, according to their own ideas, were often the proverbial "starving artists."

Even today, only a small minority of artists are able to make a living from the sale of their works. Many depend on their family's support. Another important source of income are grants from official institutions or private foundations. Also, most artists hold one or more other jobs, frequently in the art business: in exhibition design and installation, as an exhibition guard, or in art appreciation. Another traditional field of activity is teaching up-and-coming artists at art schools.

More and more artists even include their outside job in their practice of art. For example, in 1982, in the depressed area of the South Bronx in New York, the American artist Tim Rollins began to awaken an interest in literature and art among underprivileged youth in his "Art and Knowledge Workshop." Since then, working under the name Tim Rollins and K.O.S. (Kids of Survival), the artist and his collaborators have created numerous joint works that, in the meantime, have found entry into major collections and museums, such as the Tate London and the Museum of Modern Art, New York.

What is art?

“Art unlocks doors and opens new perspectives. — For me, it’s a way of expressing feelings, a bridge to understanding deeper connections, a link with the universe. — Art is the joy of experiencing strong feelings—a ticket to a world of dreams/nightmares.”

Maja Hoffmann, art patron and founder of the LUMA Foundation

Maja Hoffmann next to Olafur Eliasson’s *Berlin colour sphere,* 2006, in her London residence

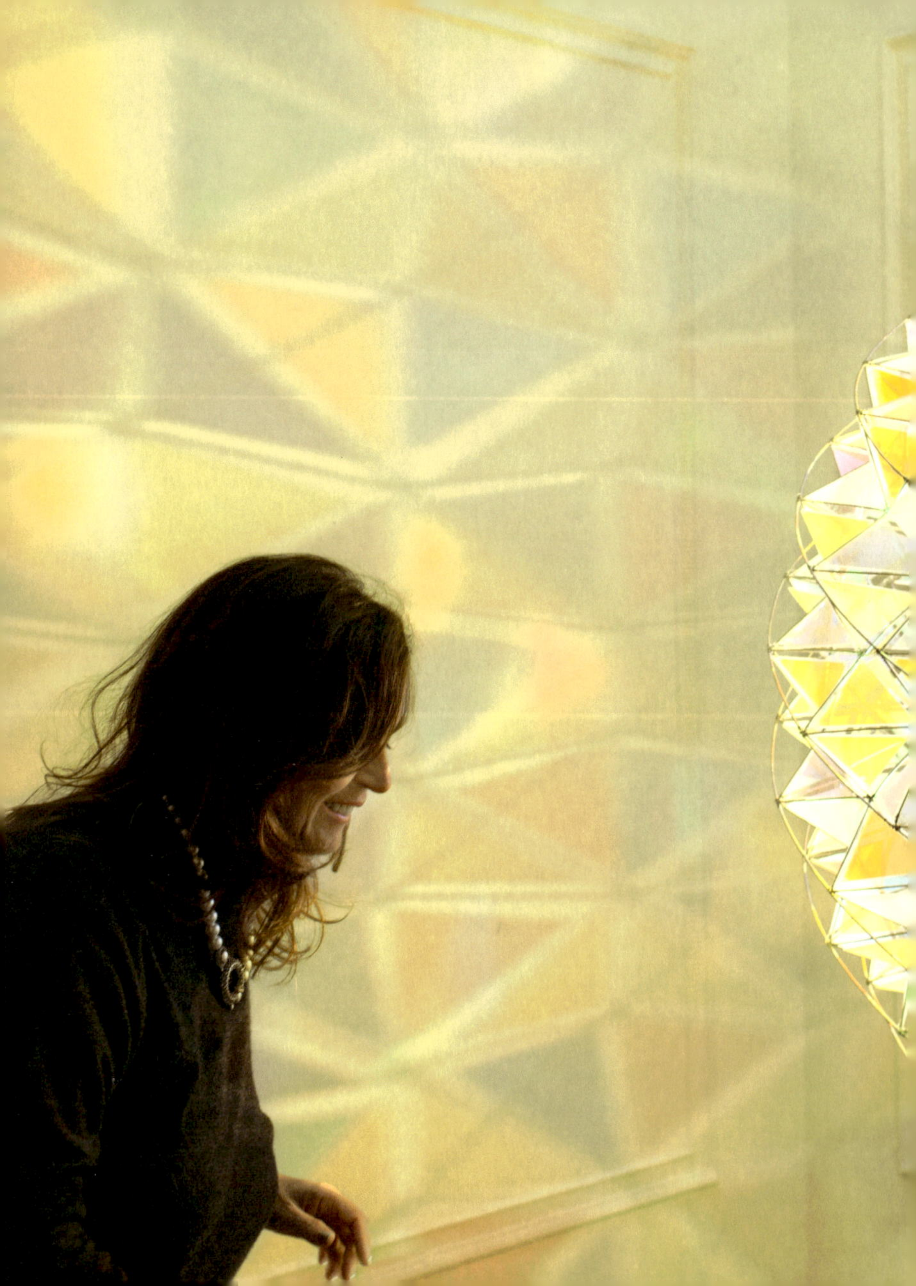

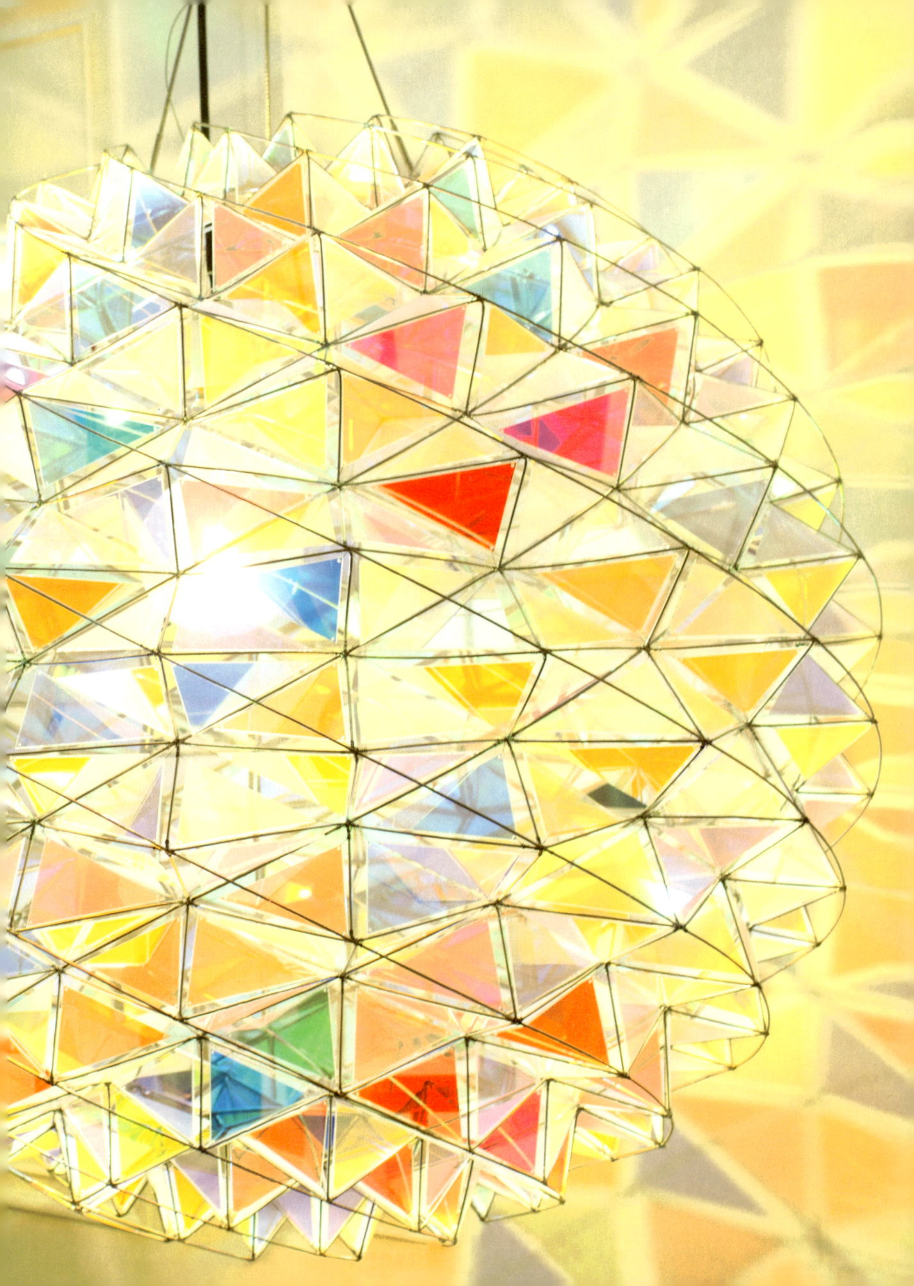

4

8

OLOR

12

STS USE

24

TEN?

8 WHAT COLOR DO ARTISTS USE MOST OFTEN?

If you ask paint suppliers, the answer is quite clear. The use of colors reflected in sales figures reveals the following color hit parade:

White is very frequently used as a ground (the first paint layer on canvas or paper) and is mixed with other colors to make them lighter.

Black, too, is used as a ground, as well as to produce black and white contrasts, contour lines, and shades of gray.

Yellow is a light color, and therefore has a low mixing strength. That is, you need a lot of yellow to produce mixed colors like green, orange, brown, etc. That is why a lot of yellow is used.

Red is an intense color with a high mixing strength. Compared with yellow, less red is needed when mixing colors.

Blue has a very high mixing strength and is therefore used in smaller amounts. Blue is often mixed with white, black, yellow, or red.

Yellow, red, and blue are the primary colors. With admixtures of black and white, an endless range of colors can be mixed from them: orange, green, brown, violet, ocher, olive green, pink, and many more.

Some artists specialize in certain colors. In the case of the young Pablo Picasso, for example, we distinguish between his "Blue Period" (from 1901) and his "Rose Period" (from 1905). The Dutch artist Piet Mondrian stopped mixing colors in the twenties and began using only the three primary colors, along with black and white. Paul Cézanne is famous, among other things, for his unique greenish-blue, and Édouard Manet for his magnificent blacks. The American Robert Ryman made countless variants of white in hundreds of paintings, and the French conceptual artist Yves Klein even invented his own color in the fifties—an ultramarine blue he had patented as "International Klein Blue." The recipe has remained a secret to this day.

What is art?

“Art is a certain way of subtly and sensitively visualizing a temporal atmosphere, with material or as expression. — Art is something immaterial, beginning with inspiration and intuition, and not necessarily a value. — It is something essential and a great asset to our culture.”

Hanspeter Marty, restorer, Kunsthaus Zürich

Hanspeter Marty inspecting Ferdinand Hodler’s painting *Truth,* 1902, Kunsthaus Zürich

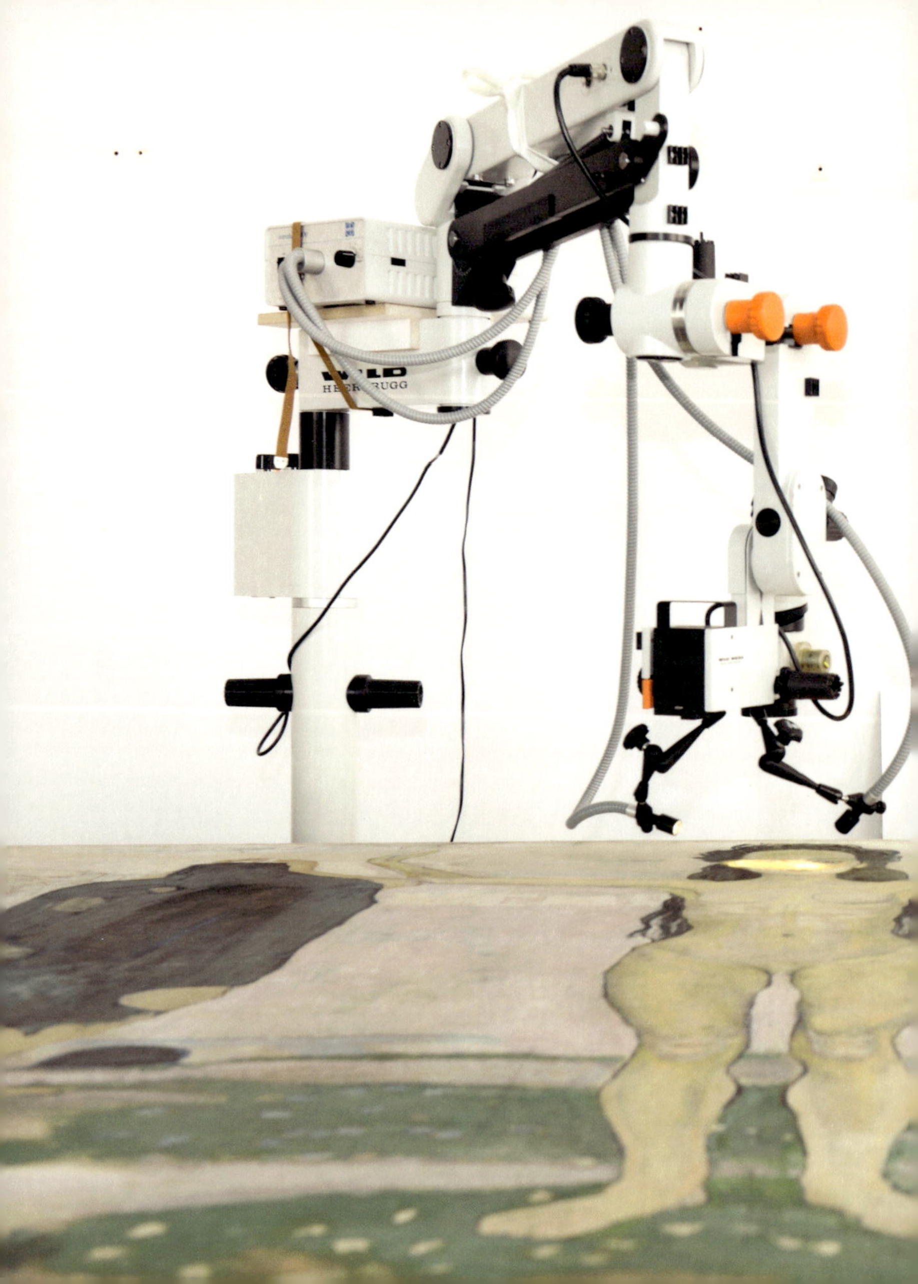

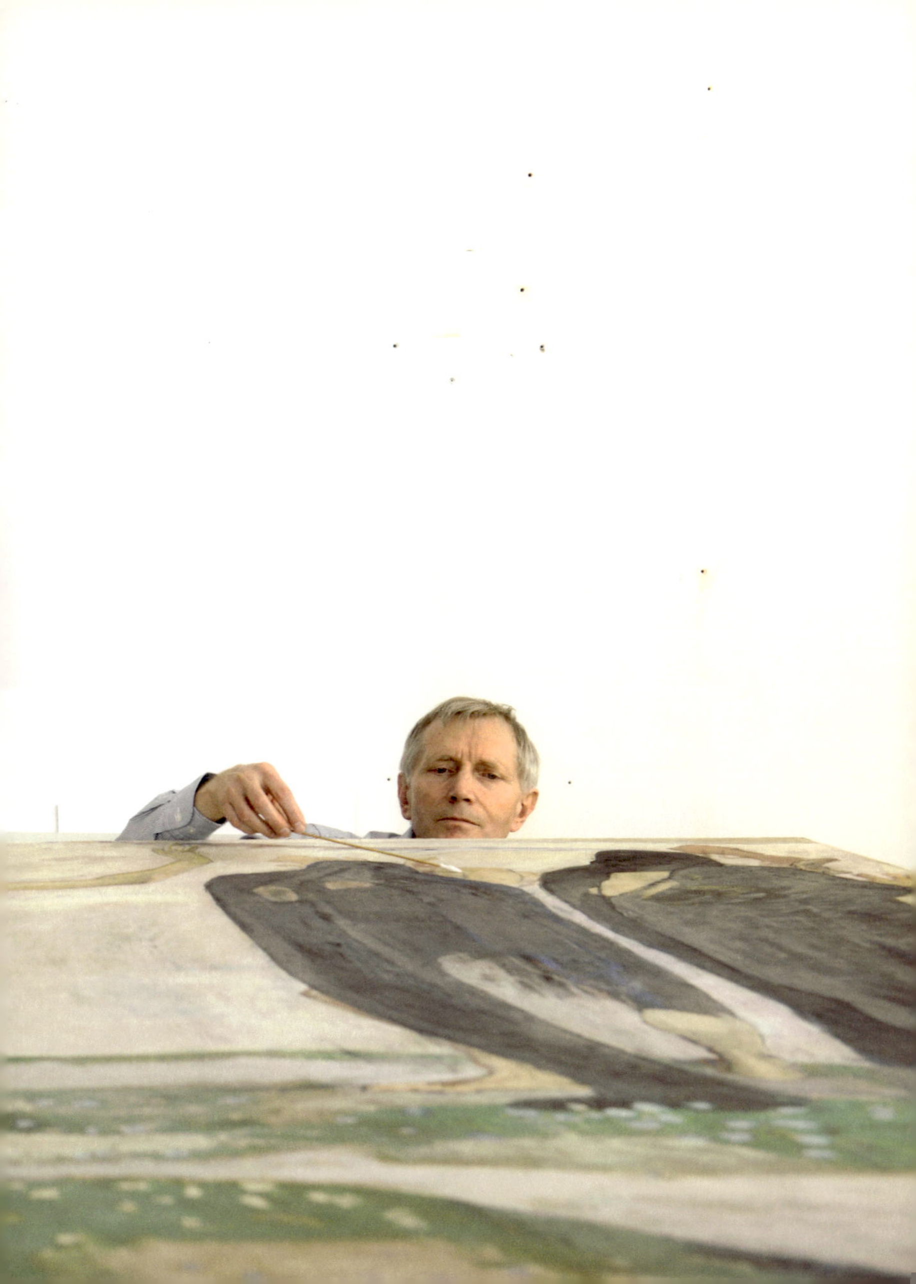

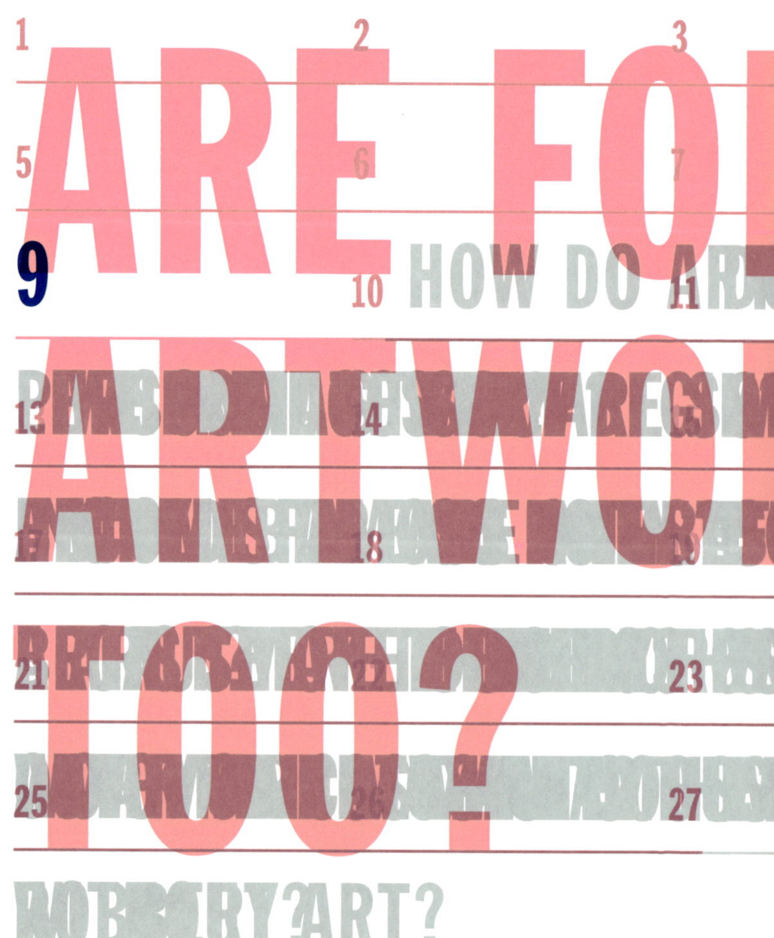

GERIES

KS,

9 ARE FORGERIES ARTWORKS, TOO?

A forgery is a swindle. It is made with the intent to deceive. We speak of a forgery when someone paints a picture that is made to look, for example, like a Dalí or a Picasso, so that it can be sold to a gullible collector for an enormous sum.

But what we expect from a work of art is that it be "original." This means that it really is by the person who signed it—or at least that it embodies his or her idea. With a forgery, this is not the case. That is why it is not a work of art.

Yet, not every painting that looks as though it were by a famous artist is automatically a forgery. Many museums contain paintings that experts long thought were done by the Dutch master Rembrandt. Ever since 1968, when the Rembrandt Research Project began to test the authenticity of the countless Rembrandts around the world, the number of real Rembrandts has decreased by more than a third. Now only about 320 works are considered original; the rest are probably from the artist's workshop, done by pupils, or copies made by later artists. These are not forgeries because, in Rembrandt's day, it was customary to have workshop assistants and pupils help masters satisfy the great demand for paintings. In addition, copying was an important part of artistic training, and it was an acceptable method of reproducing a popular work, because photography was an invention that still lay far in the future.

It was not until the late nineteenth century that art historians began to distinguish between individual artists by making critical comparisons. A good example in Germany is the famous "Holbein dispute." At the time, there were two almost identical depictions of the Virgin, one in Dresden and the other in Darmstadt, both of which were thought to be by the Renaissance painter Hans Holbein the Younger. Both cities claimed to own the original. Yet, the Dresden Virgin was long considered more beautiful, and thus more masterly and authentic, by many art lovers. By comparing it with other Holbein works, art historians finally decided that the Dresden picture must be a copy that was made a good hundred years after the original.

Copies of paintings by famous artists are still made today. For little money, we can order a "Dalí" in oil on canvas anytime on the internet. As long as the seller does not declare the painting to be an original, it cannot be called a forgery.

Visitor in front of Pablo Picasso's sculpture *Woman with Hat,* 1961/63,
Fondation Beyeler, Riehen/Basel

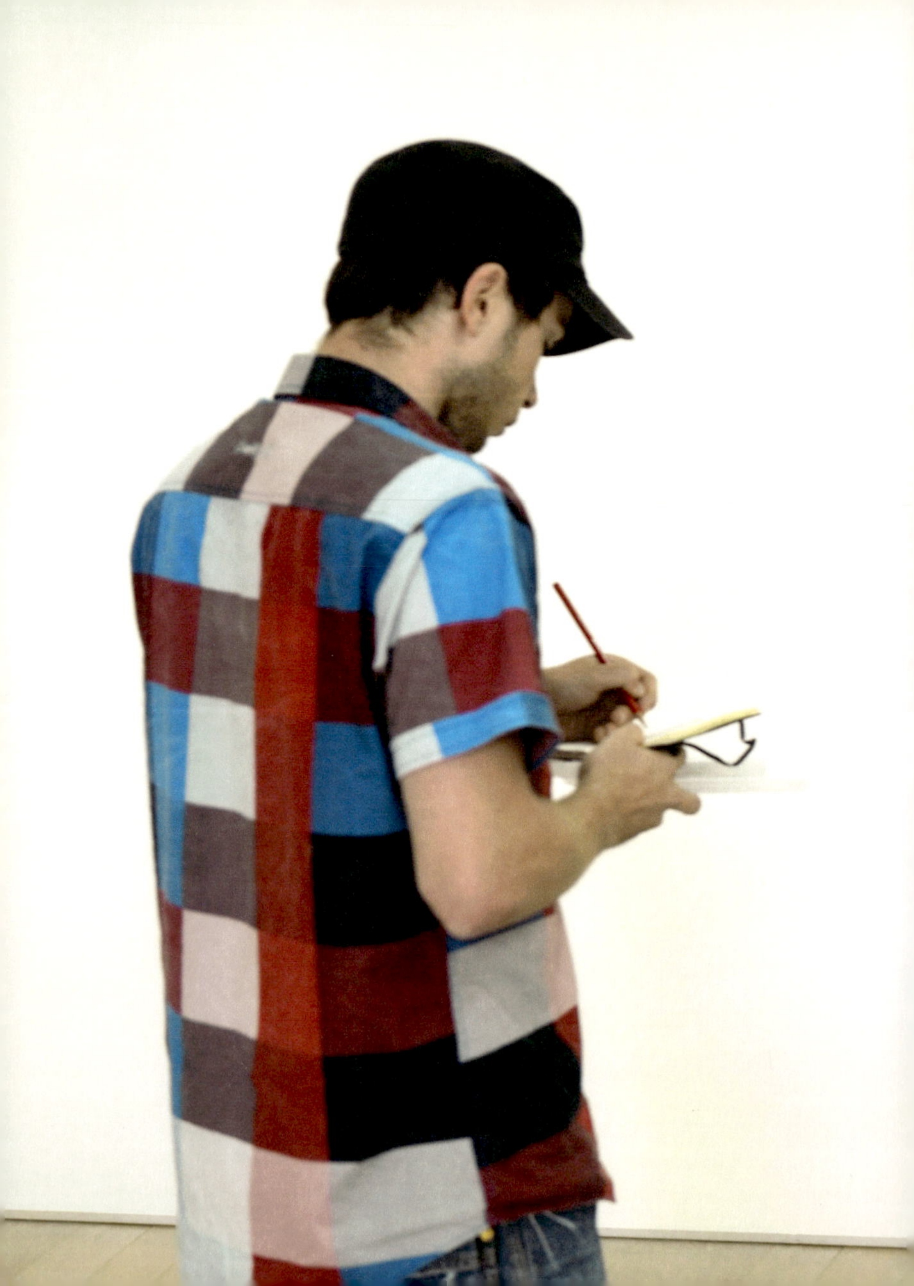

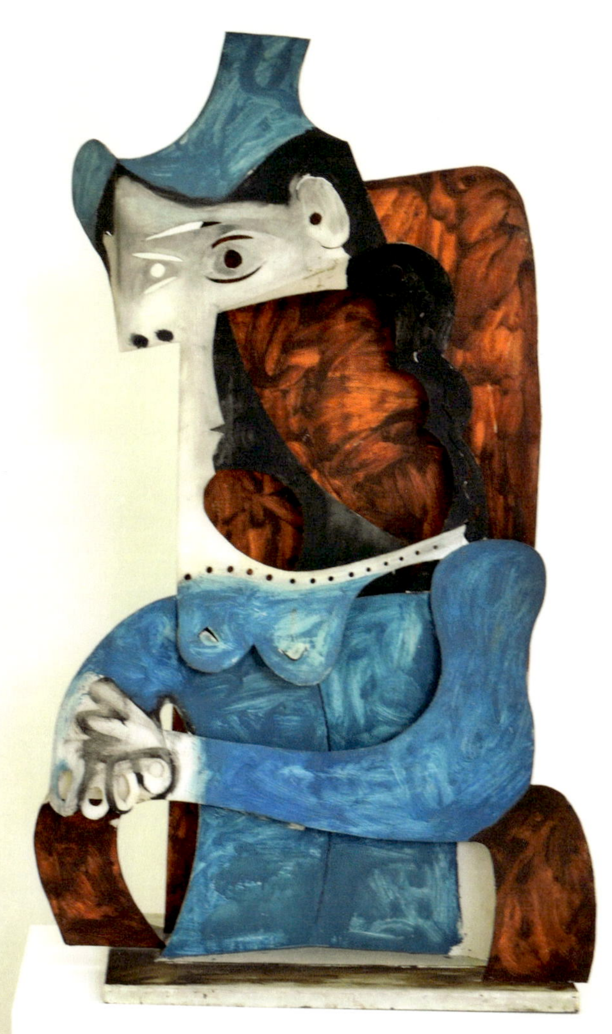

HOW DO ARTISTS WELL-KN

10

ART?

4

8

ECOME

12

16

WN?

20

24

10 HOW DO ARTISTS BECOME WELL-KNOWN?

An artist's career is determined by a wide variety of factors:

Training — Most artists study at an academy or art school. They generally have their first exhibitions there, which may attract the attention of gallery owners.

Galleries — Galleries work like agencies. When dealers find the work of an artist interesting, they attempt to sell it.

Art fairs — At art fairs, many galleries come together to offer the work of the artists they represent. Art fairs are held in many countries, but the largest and most influential is Art Basel, in Switzerland. It attracts collectors and curators from around the world who wish to inform themselves about the latest developments or buy works.

Art criticism — In earlier times, it was mainly art critics whose reviews of exhibitions in newspapers shaped public opinion and thus artists' careers. A good example is the critic Clement Greenberg, thanks to whose support the painter Jackson Pollock became a superstar on the American art scene in the fifties.

Curators — Nowadays, curators are as influential as art critics used to be. They are the people who decide what art is presented to a broad public in museum exhibitions.

Biennales — Biennales are large overview exhibitions that show approaches to art from around the world every two years. The longest-running and most famous is the Venice Biennale. In addition to biennales, there are shows that are held every three or four years. The most important exhibition held at five-year intervals is the documenta, in Kassel, Germany. Any artist selected to participate steps into the international spotlight.

Collections — For an artist to become truly well-known, as many of his or her works as possible must find entry into major collections—whether they be held by private art lovers or by large corporations. Acceptance into a museum collection amounts to a seal of quality.

This list naturally makes no claim to completeness. There are at least three more factors that are necessary for success in the art world: hard work, social skills, and being lucky enough to be in the right place at the right time!

What is art?

"Louise Bourgeois, a great friend and brilliant artist, once said: 'I am not what I am, I am what I do with my hands.' Art is a means to explore one's identity. What's incredible is that this can be an individual identity, a national identity, or even the identity of an entire generation. In the broadest sense, art can bring together a community and, on a personal level, it can shed light on one's most intimate thoughts. Art lives from the fact that it remains unexplainable, and that is what distinguishes it from science."

Iwan Wirth, gallery owner, Galerie Hauser & Wirth, Zurich and London

Iwan Wirth with Mary Heilmann's works *Rietveld-Remix #3,* 2012, and *Good Vibrations Diptych, Remembering David,* 1992–2011, in the London branch of Hauser & Wirth

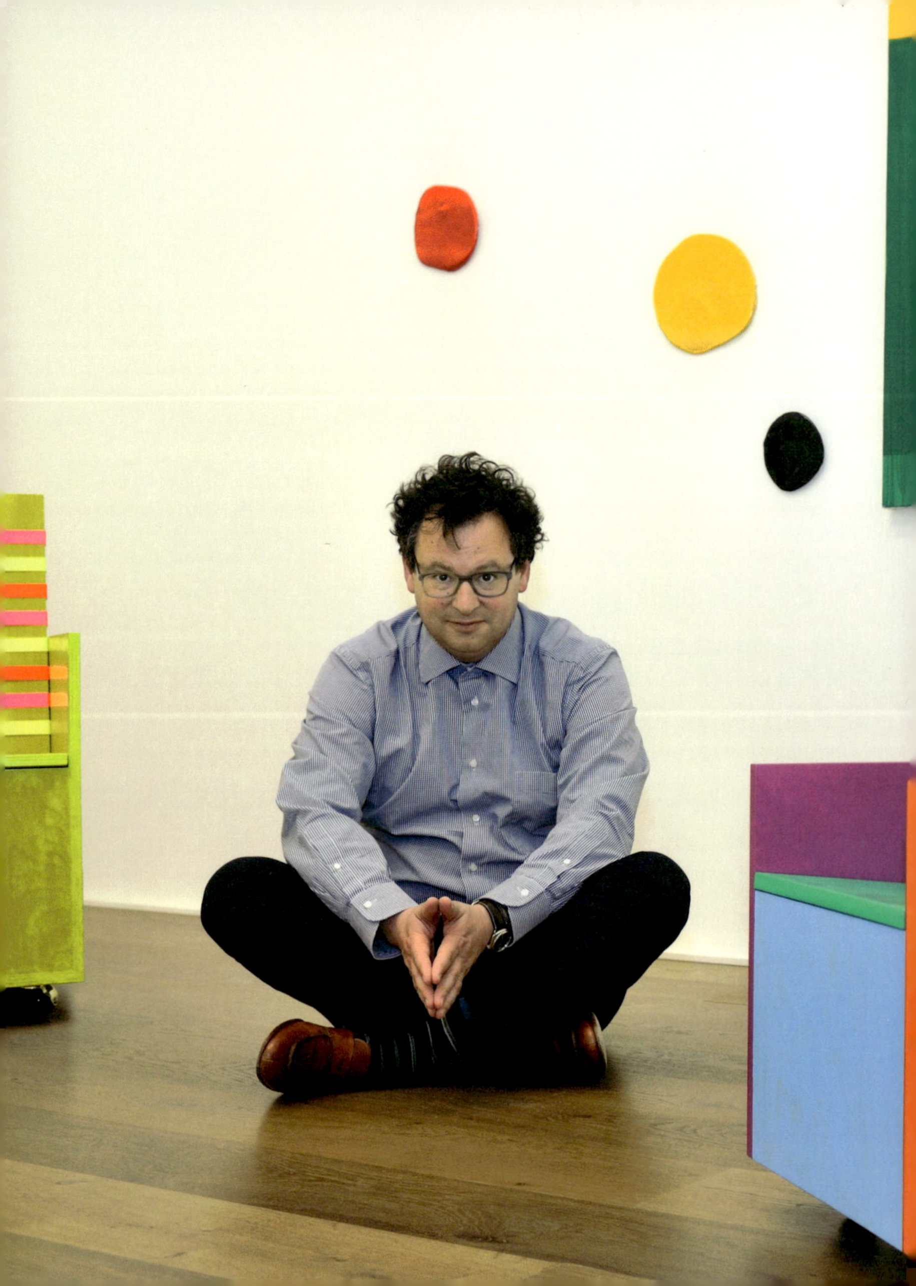

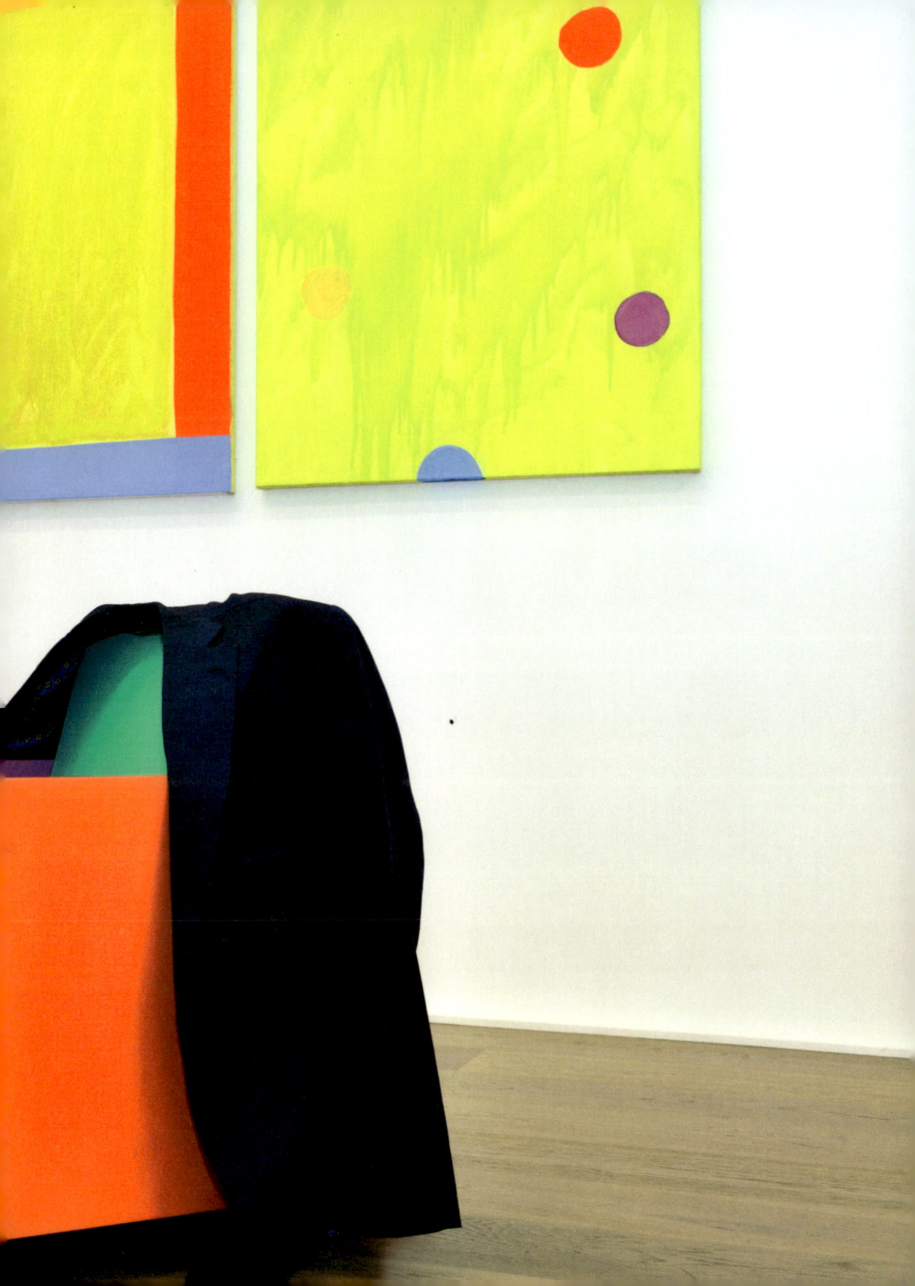

DOES EV
ARTIST H
11
A PERSO
STYLE?

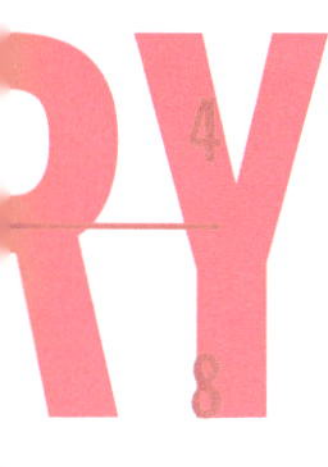

11 DOES EVERY ARTIST HAVE A PERSONAL STYLE?

The word "style" means something like a personal touch. In other words, an artist's style basically refers to the individual, recognizable way in which he or she shapes the materials at hand.

Time and again artists have become known for their unusual style. Around 1600, for example, the Italian Caravaggio developed a new type of "light-and-dark" painting that made his pictures immediately recognizable. He was so successful that young painters, even in other countries, began to imitate Caravaggio's style. So the word "style" can also refer to a very special way of painting, drawing, or modeling that is shared by a number of artists. In retrospect, attempts are even made to detect styles common to entire eras. We speak of the Gothic, the Renaissance, or the Baroque style. By the beginning of the twentieth century, however, such stylistic distinctions had become more and more difficult to make. In a very short time, many different styles and artistic movements emerged in Europe: Expressionism, Cubism, Constructivism, etc. They developed in part at the same time and, in some cases, the same artists were involved.

Today, in contemporary art, there are so many different stances, strategies, and approaches that we can no longer speak of styles as names for epochs.

In spite of this, an idea that's still widespread is that good artists must establish their personal style at an early age and remain true to it from then on. A recognizably original style is, after all, very important in order to be successful on the art market. Richard Serra conforms perfectly to this idea. After switching from painting to sculpture as a young man, Serra first tried out materials like rubber and lead, then turned entirely to steel. Since the seventies, he has produced impressive steel sculptures of enormous dimensions. The sculptor Louise Bourgeois is a famous counter-example to Serra. She has often been accused of having no personal style at all. During the course of her career, Bourgeois employed a wide range of sculptural materials, using traditional marble and bronze as well as experimenting with latex and textiles. She made small-scale drawings as well as monumental installations. Up until the end of her life, Bourgeois tirelessly pursued new paths.

What is art?

"That's something I, too, would like to know, what art is. Today, the boundaries are more open than ever before. Art is everywhere. There are lots of artworks and opinions. And still, it takes an entire life to create great art that catches the eye, moves the mind and soul for longer than a human lifetime. It communicates a message and leads you into its own reality. You have to discover it."

Margrit Hahnloser, collector, Zurich

Margrit Hahnloser among works from her collection: Jasper Johns's *Passage I—Working Proof,* 1966 (front); Xerxes Ach's *Painting,* 2008 (back left); Donald Baechler's *Inexplicable Gift,* 2003 (back right); and Tim Scott's *From Matisse II,* 1981

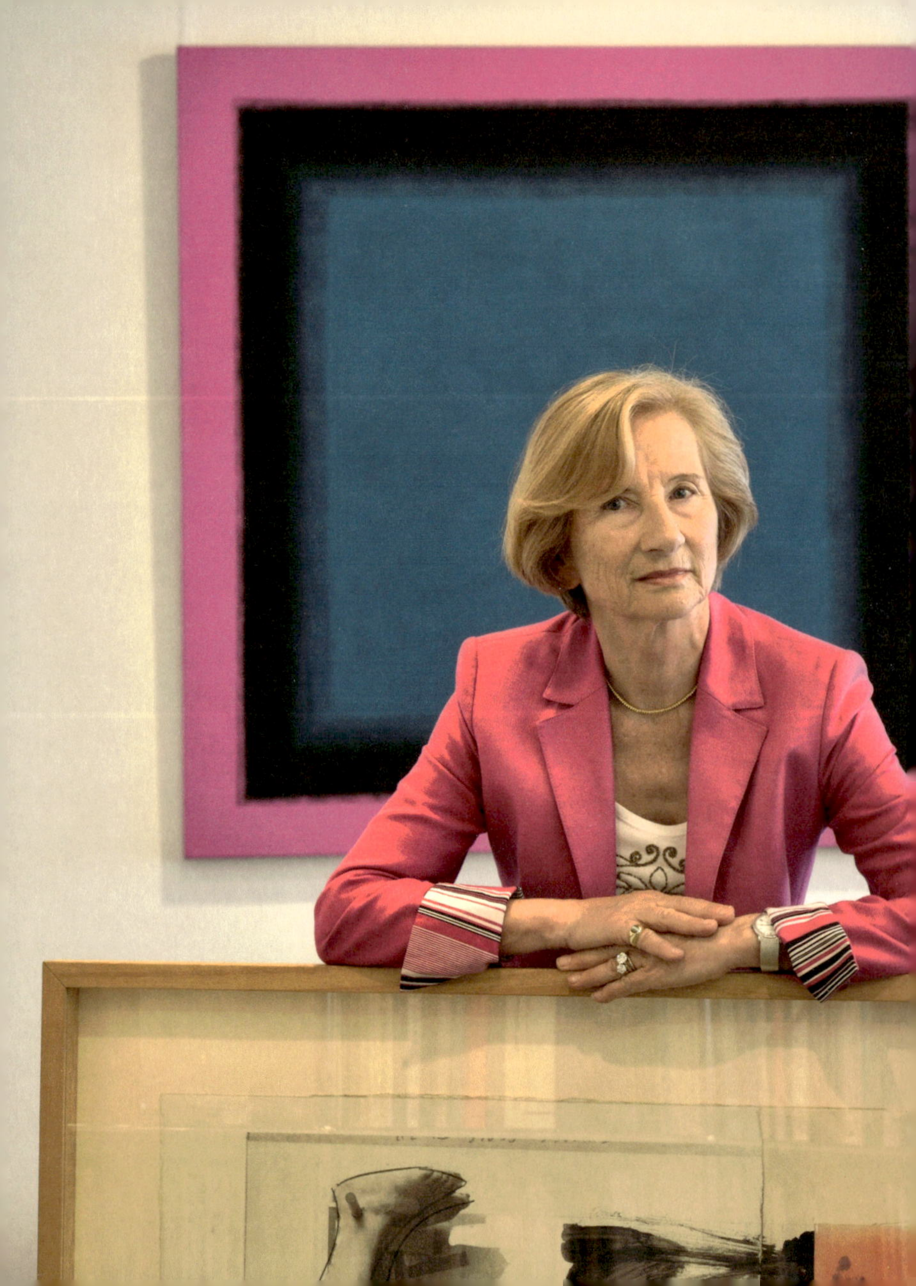

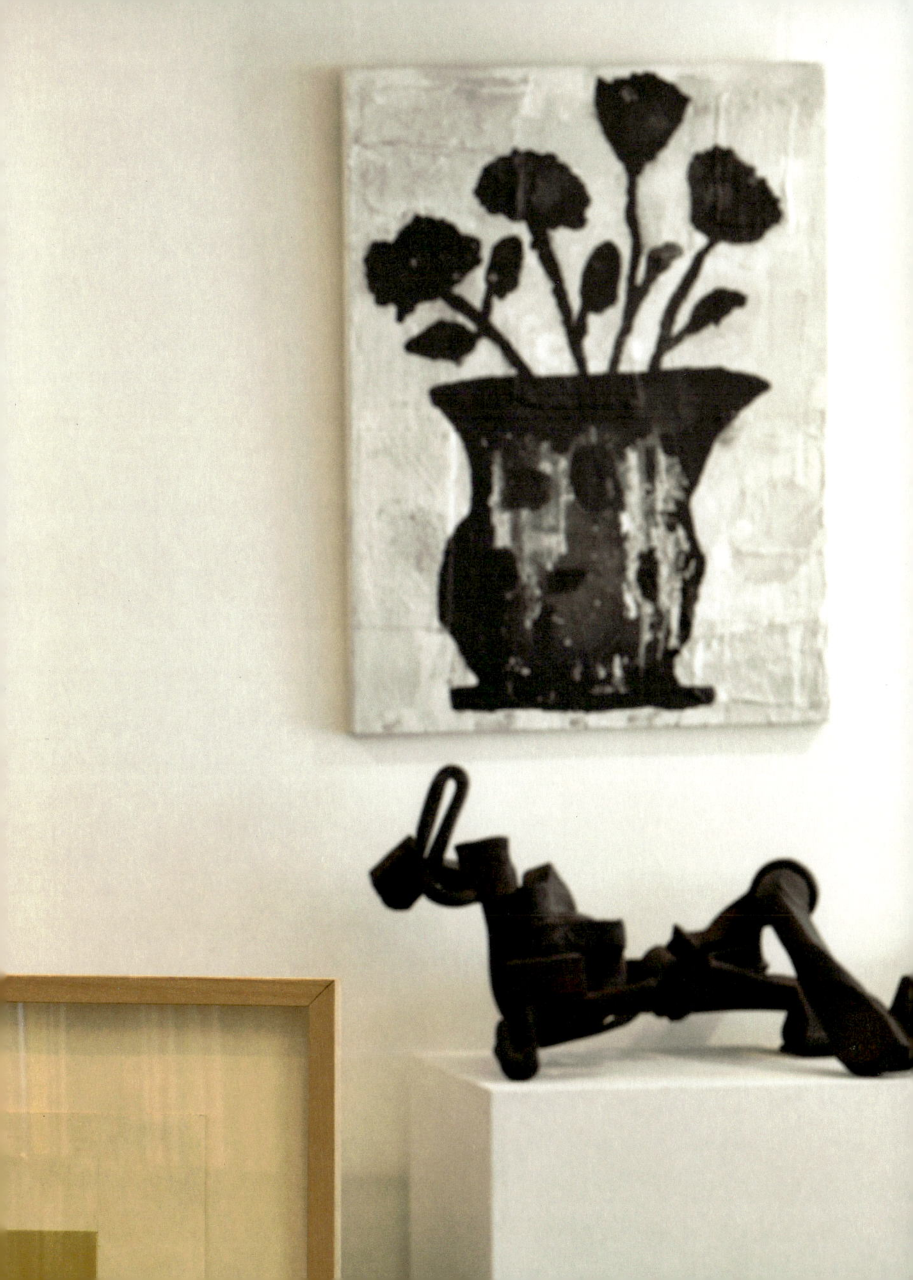

DID ANDY WA

LIKE TOMATO

WHERE DOES

ART?

1 2 3

5 6 7

9 10 11

13 14 15

17 18 19

21 22 23

25 26 27

HOL.

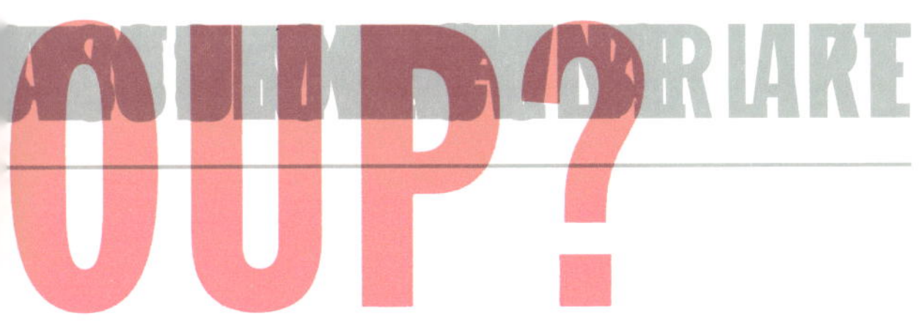

12 DID ANDY WARHOL LIKE TOMATO SOUP?

"I used to drink it. I used to have the same lunch every day, for twenty years, I guess, the same thing over and over again."

Andy Warhol (1928–1987) says he had Campbell's soup for lunch year after year, no doubt including the tomato soup that would become one of his most famous motifs. Whether or not he particularly liked Campbell's tomato soup, we can't be entirely sure. But it was probably the best-known variety of Campbell's when he turned it into a work of art. Warhol devoted himself especially to things that every American child saw every day—at the supermarket, on TV, in advertising. Or to pop stars like the actress Marilyn Monroe and First Lady Jackie Kennedy, whose pictures people saw so often they thought they knew them, even though they had never actually met.

While many other famous painters also began to design posters or objects of everyday life in the course of their career, Warhol took the opposite path. He worked as a commercial artist and window-display designer before turning to the visual arts. He made silkscreen, a technique used in the commercial fields of publishing and advertising, into an accepted method of creating art. It enabled him to mass-produce popular motifs. In his work *Thirty Are Better than One,* he lined up *Mona Lisas* in rows like the soup cans, and he even went so far as to print dollar bills on canvas. The studio where he made his art with the help of many assistants was called "The Factory," and his signature "Andy Warhol" became a trademark.

Warhol remains a mystery to art historians even today. Was he secretly a critic of consumerism who wanted to show that art in capitalism is a commodity like everything else that is produced, sold, and consumed? That the *Mona Lisa* and a soup can are no different in kind? Was he a democratic artist who used banal motifs to knock art off its high pedestal and make it accessible to all? Or was he just a clever businessman who exploited the tastes of the masses for his own advancement?

One thing is certain: there was never any better advertising for Campbell's soup than Warhol's paintings.

Security guard and Andy Warhol's *Large Campbell's Soup Can,* 1964, in the conference room of Campbell Soup Company, Camden, New Jersey

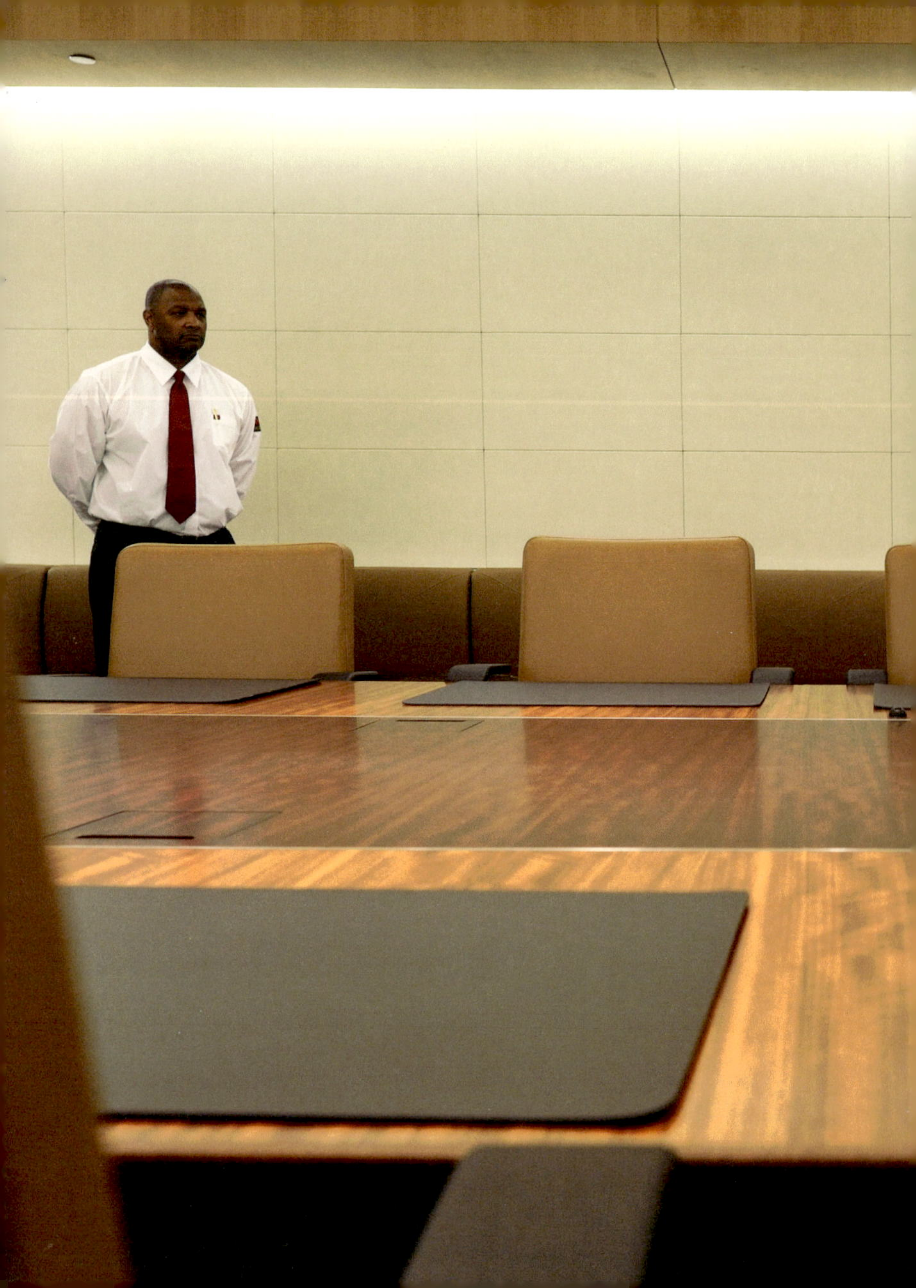

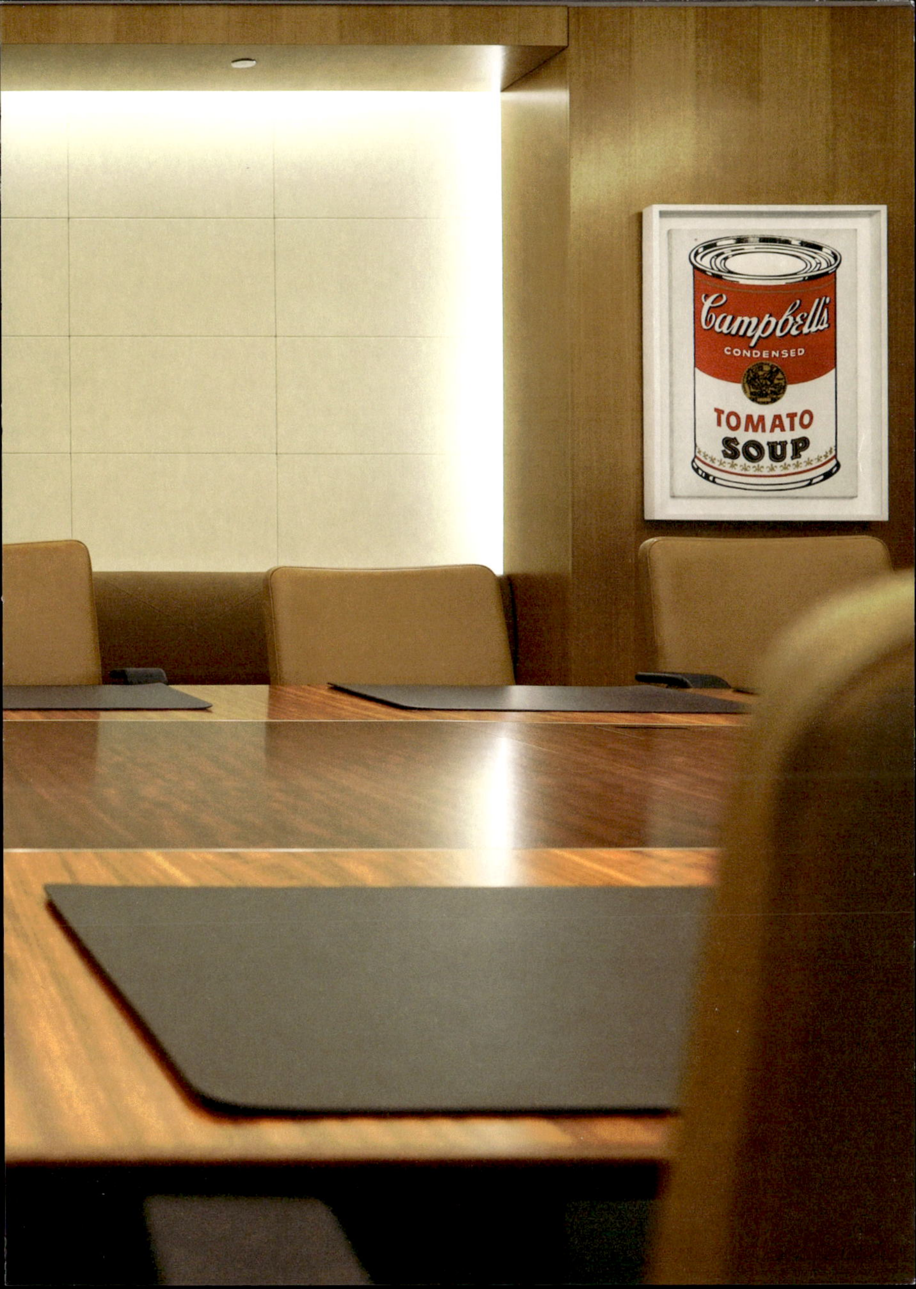
Campbell's
CONDENSED
TOMATO
SOUP

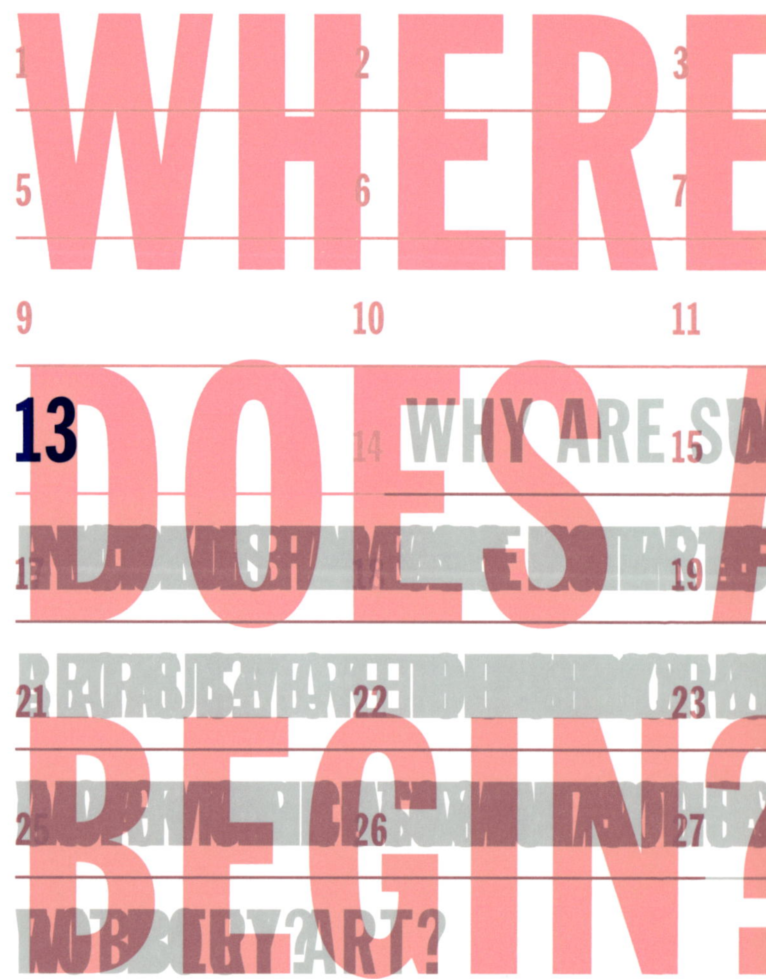
WHERE
DOES A
BEGIN?
13
WHY ARE SU
ART?

13 WHERE DOES ART BEGIN?

Let's imagine ourselves in times long past, hearing the first song ever sung, seeing the first picture, the first drawing, the first sculpture ever made…

Did people in ancient cultures even speak of art, or did they think more in terms of acts and rituals? Was the act more important than the finished "art" product?

Cave paintings — The oldest pictures in human history are found in the Chauvet cave in southern France. These cave paintings, more than 30,000 years old, were discovered in 1994 in the rugged Ardèche canyon. We can only imagine what their authors—be they artists, hunters, or shamans—might have been thinking or feeling when they made them in primeval times. Yet, we can study their works. When we look at them through modern eyes, we—admiringly—call them "art."

Our personal story of the beginning — Looking back over our own life, we can ask ourselves when and where we first came into contact with art. The beginning is not easy to determine because there is much that escapes our memory. Only a few key childhood experiences—positive or negative—stick in our mind: a favorite picture book, for example, or climbing on a sculpture in the park, or the picture hanging above our grandparents' sofa. One thing is certain, though:

that we experience art in many shapes long before we even know what the word “art” means.

Another art story — Let’s imagine the very first scribbles that a child makes. Maybe it’s not yet art. But when the child grows older and keeps on drawing, it could be that his or her drawings become works of art.

In 1902, the painter Paul Klee, then aged twenty-two, discovered some of his own children’s drawings in his parents’ attic in Bern. In his eyes, they were very much on the same level as his “adult” pictures, so he included them in his list of works and showed them in a Berlin exhibition. Where is the borderline between art and non-art in this case? The boundary is permeable. Both artists and art lovers continually redefine where art begins—and this has been going on for millennia.

Visitor in Sergio Prego’s installation *Ikurriña Quarter,* 2010, at the booth of the Galería Soledad Lorenzo at *Art Unlimited,* Art 41 Basel, 2010

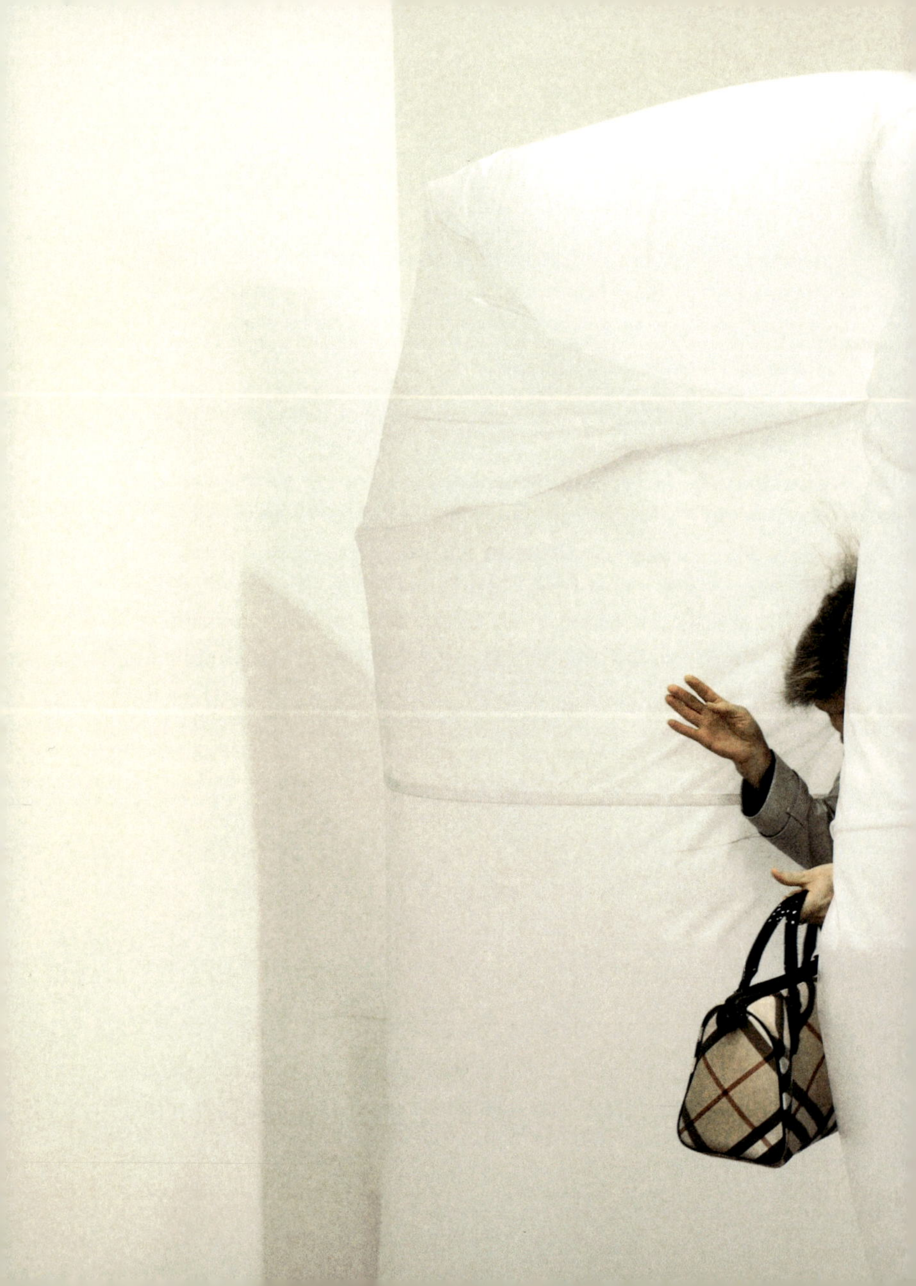

WHY ARE
WORKS O
SO INCRE
EXPENSIV

SOME

ART

IBLY

?

14 WHY ARE SOME WORKS OF ART SO INCREDIBLY EXPENSIVE?

Artworks often change hands for breathtakingly large sums of money. When, in May 2004, the one-hundred-million-dollar mark for a painting was surpassed for the first time, it was a sensation. How does a price like this come about?

Here are some of the criteria that determine sales prices:

Artists' reputations — The more famous an artist is, the more expensive his or her works are.

Familiarity with the works — Pictures that have been shown in major exhibitions or publications are considered to be especially valuable.

Status or quality of an artist's lifework — All artists pass through various phases in the course of their development. Their unique high points and major works are considered particularly valuable.

Origin — If a work of art has an especially interesting "provenance," that is, a special origin or history (a famous former owner, for example), this is viewed as increasing its value.

Rarity — Rare or "one-off" works are in very high demand.

Authenticity — The authenticity of a work should always be confirmed by an expert's opinion. Even the slightest doubt about whether it's an original can lead to a massive loss in value.

Freshness — When a work has seldom changed hands and has never (or not recently) been offered for sale, it is considered "fresh," making it highly attractive for the art market.

State of preservation — A work's condition should naturally be good. Even if the work is decades or even centuries old, it should neither be damaged nor darkened or faded.

Marketing — Clever advertising for a work of art can increase its ideal value and sales price.

Trends — What people like or don't like, what artist is currently "in" or "out," is determined for the most part by the zeitgeist, that is, by fashion trends.

Economic situation — When a lot of money is in circulation and many wealthy art lovers are buying art, the prices increase.

Supply and demand — When two people at an art auction both want to buy the same work, it goes to the highest bidder. Supply and demand, and sheer buying power, determine the price of an artwork in the end.

What is art?

"Art is being able to define the word art! — For me, the best definition is Groucho Marx's. When asked 'What is art?' he replied, 'The abbreviation for Arthur.' — We don't need art in order to live, but we can't live without it."

Simon de Pury, auctioneer, Phillips de Pury & Company, New York and London

Simon de Pury next to Tim Noble & Sue Webster's *Puny Undernourished Kid* and *Girlfriend from Hell* (diptych), both 2004, in the New York auction rooms of Phillips de Pury & Company

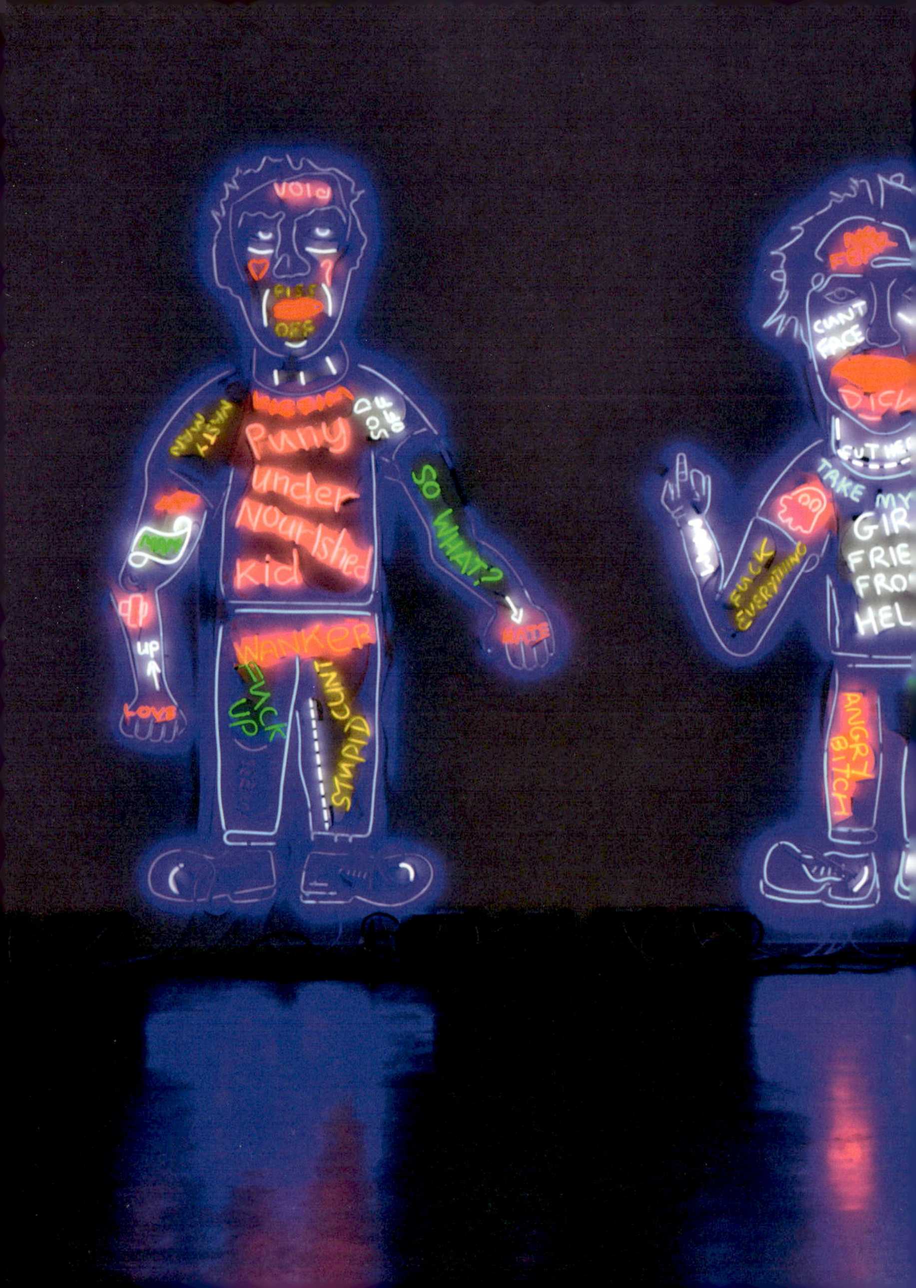

VOID
PISS OFF
NASTY MAN
Puny under Nourished kid
SO WHAT?
up
WANKER
FUCK UP
STUPID CUNT
FEAR
CUNT FACE
TAKE MY
FUCK EVERYTHING
ANGRY BITCH

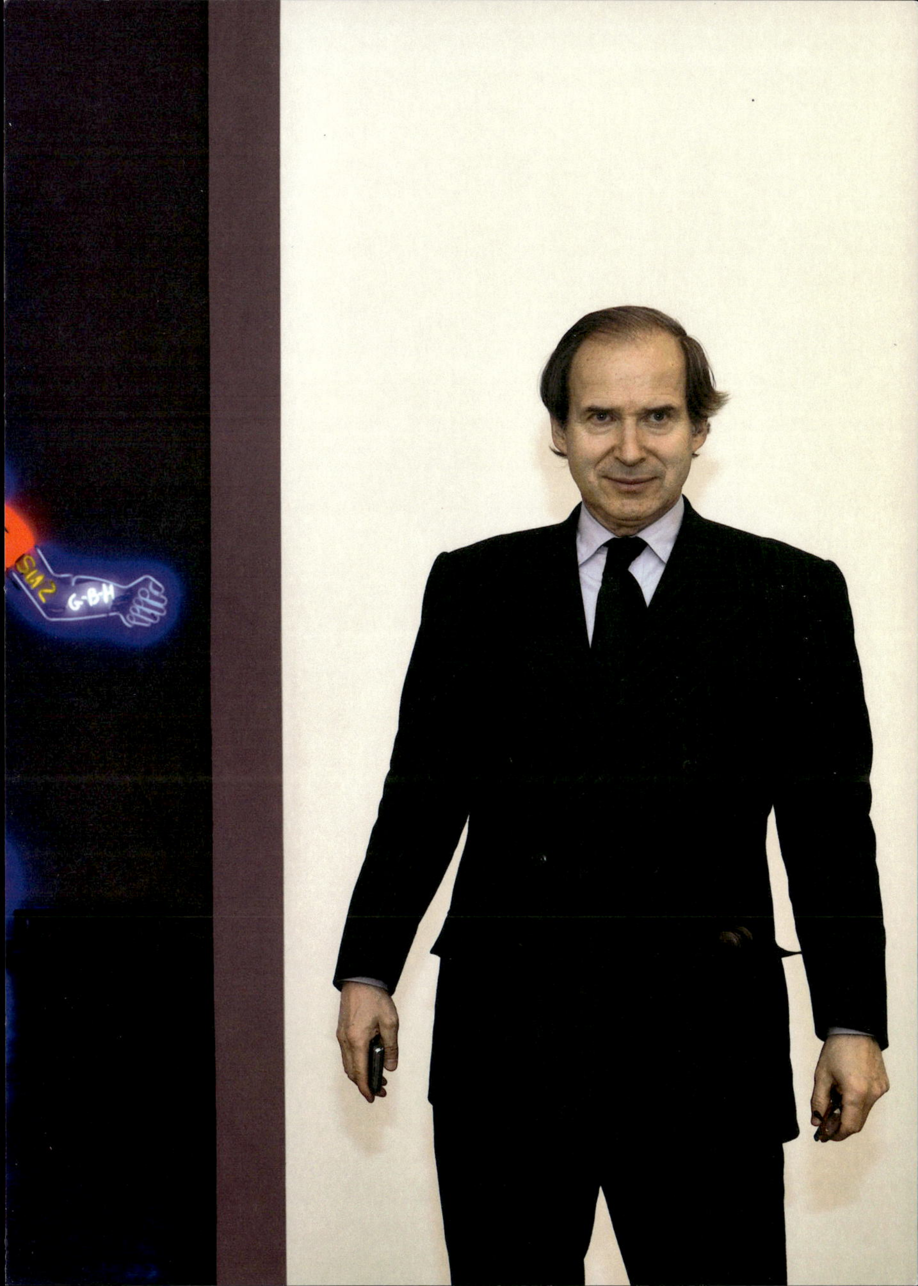
SW2
G-B-H

WHY DO SO
ARTISTS BE
FAMOUS O
THEIR DEA

1 2 3

5 6 7

9 10 11

13 14 15

17 18 19

21 22 23

25 26 27

ART?

MANY

COME

LY AFTER

H?

4

8

12

16

20

24

WHAT'S MODERN

15 WHY DO SO MANY ARTISTS BECOME FAMOUS ONLY AFTER THEIR DEATH?

Becoming famous has to do with recognition, which takes a lot of time. As a rule, fame and honor do not come overnight. In the case of some artists, it takes decades to become well-known regionally, nationally, and, finally, internationally. A large number of artists die before they are appreciated and acknowledged, such as Vincent van Gogh and Henri Rousseau.

Van Gogh shot himself in the chest in 1890, thus putting an end to his life at the age of thirty-seven. He had sold only very few pictures during his lifetime. The only people who valued his paintings were his brother and a few of his closest friends, the majority of whom were fellow artists. For most people at the time, his works were simply impossible to understand. His landscapes were depicted on canvas in brilliant colors and wild brushstrokes. Everything seemed exaggerated: the brushstrokes had a disturbing effect and the heavily applied paint was simply overwhelming.

Henri Rousseau's story is also remarkable. In Paris at the end of the nineteenth century, he was made fun of and denounced. Journalists wrote that he painted like a child and his pictures were bad jokes. Rousseau collected these biting reviews, which attacked not only his art but him personally, and carefully pasted them into an album. During the last five years of his life, Rousseau finally found recognition. Yet, he didn't become really famous until after his death. Beginning in 1910, memorial exhibitions were held in New York, Paris, and Munich. First books about him made his achievements known, art dealers began to show an interest in his work, and his paintings were acquired by major private collectors. Artists like Picasso, Delaunay, and Kandinsky also bought Rousseau's paintings, particularly because they were so different from everything that had come before. In 1936, twenty-six years after his death, Rousseau's jungle picture *The Snake Charmer* found its way into the Louvre, the most famous art museum in the world.

Rousseau and van Gogh, two crass outsiders, managed to set new standards in painting. Their pictures, only recently thought odd and badly painted, suddenly became models for imitation. Over the years, viewers' perceptions changed as their eyes became used to the unusual and the unfamiliar. People began to praise works that shortly before had been harshly criticized. Suddenly, they were seen as beautiful, gripping, or simply works of genius. Today, van Gogh and Rousseau are considered masters, and their paintings are displayed in the most important museums in the world—as well as reproduced in schoolbooks, on postcards, and in calendars.

Young man in front of Henri Rousseau's *The Hungry Lion Attacking an Antilope,* 1898/1905, Fondation Beyeler, Riehen/Basel

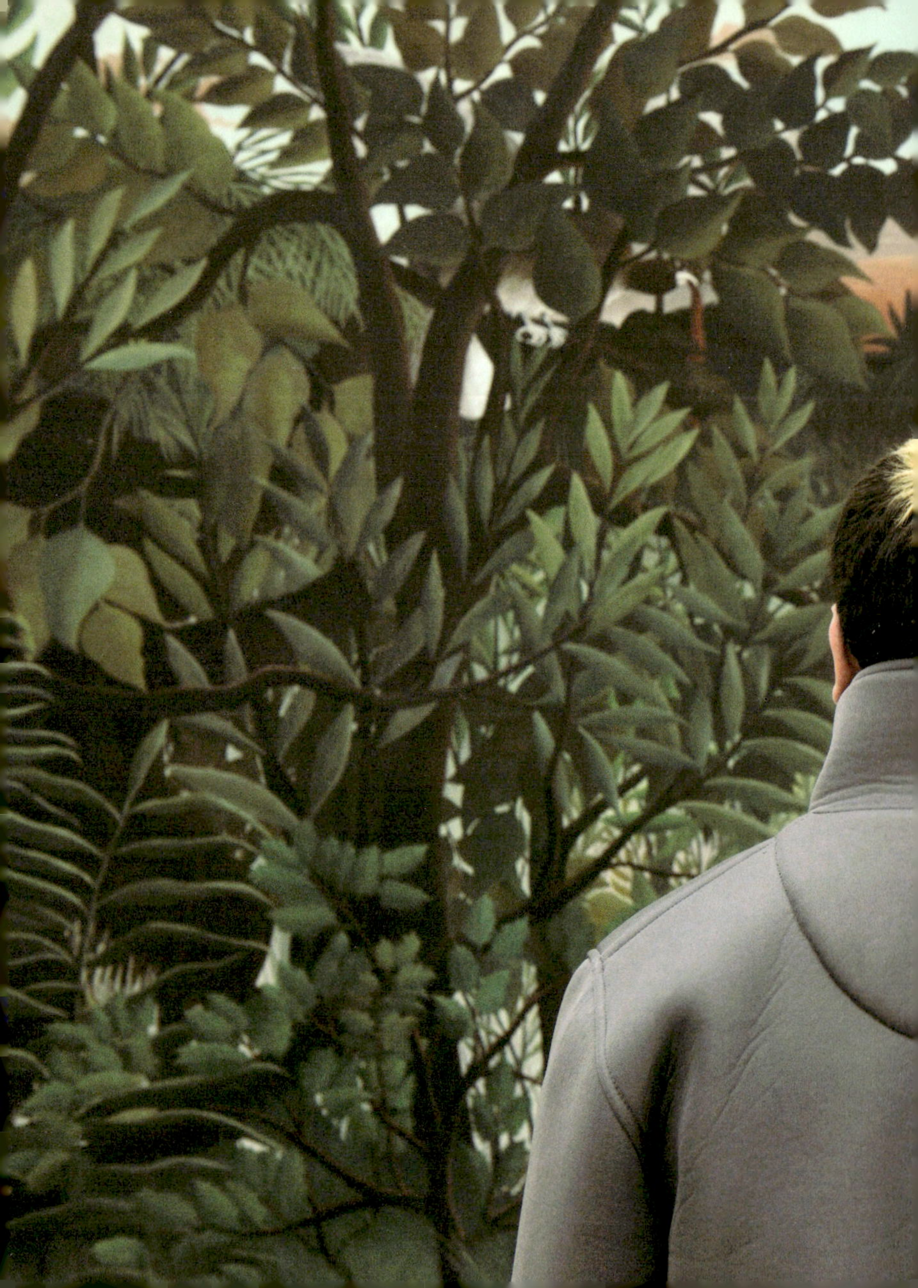

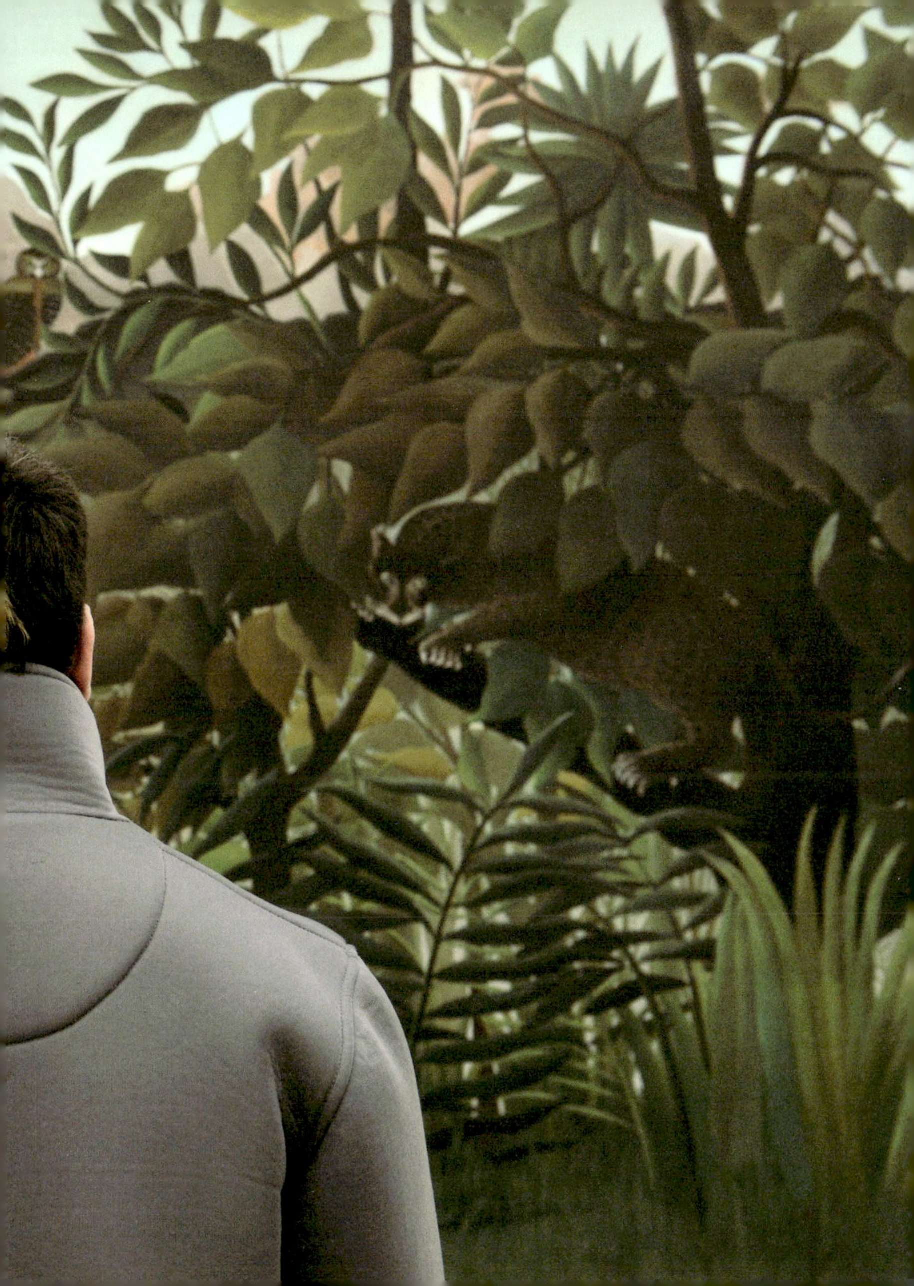

What is art?

“Everything that has yet to be named with the aid of language or imagined with the help of what is known can be made visible in art. This is why art often has an alienating effect, and is sometimes even disturbing. Yet, due to its strangeness, at the same time, it exerts a fascinating attraction and challenges the viewer over and over again. Because art brings dimensions into view that have been defined neither intellectually nor linguistically, this makes it so difficult to approach, perceive, and describe its sensuous, material nature. This is why art stands not only for a place that invites dreaming and thinking but for a mystery that can awaken our curiosity about the world.”

Claudia Blümle, Professor of Aesthetics and Art Studies, Kunstakademie Münster

Claudia Blümle viewing slides at the Kunstakademie Münster

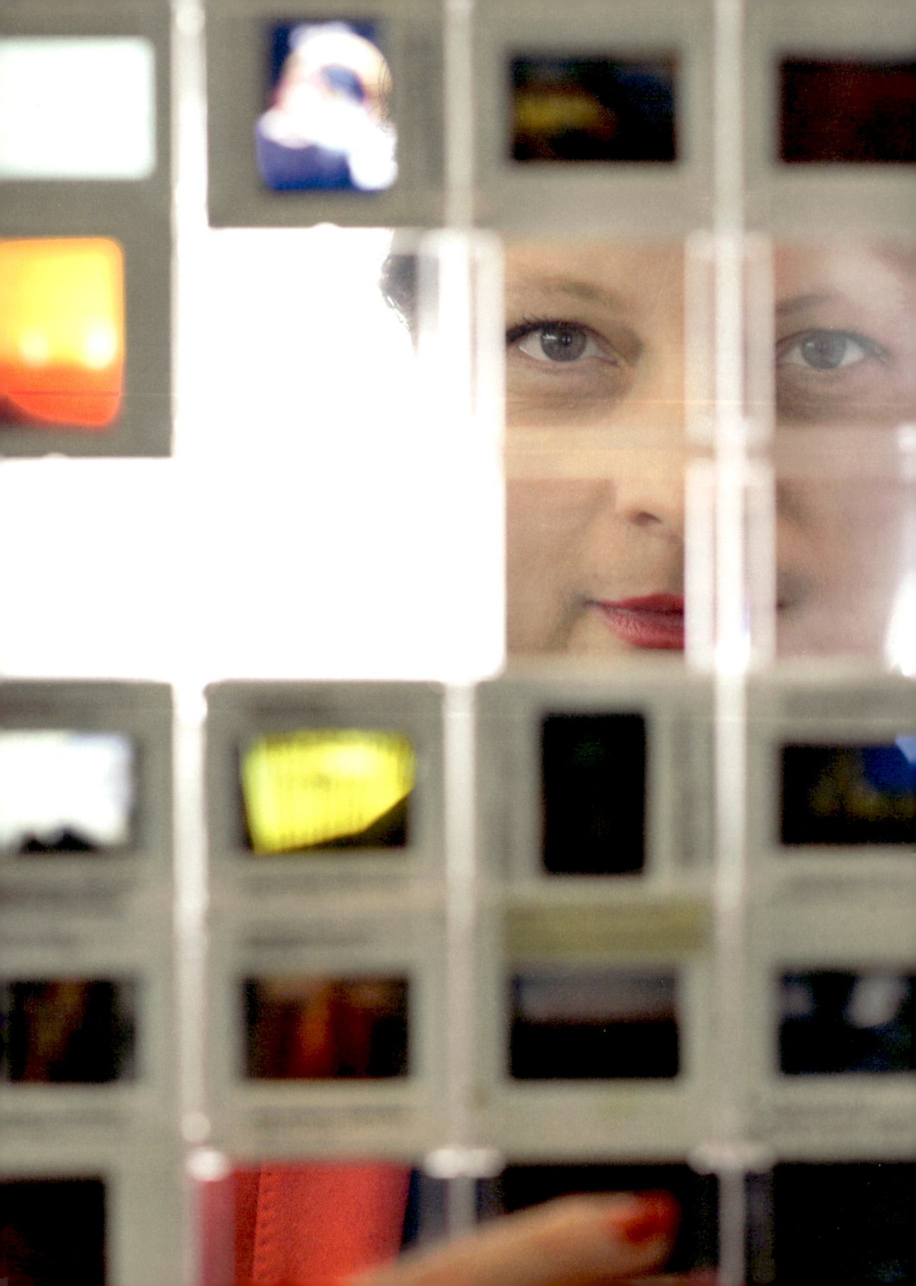

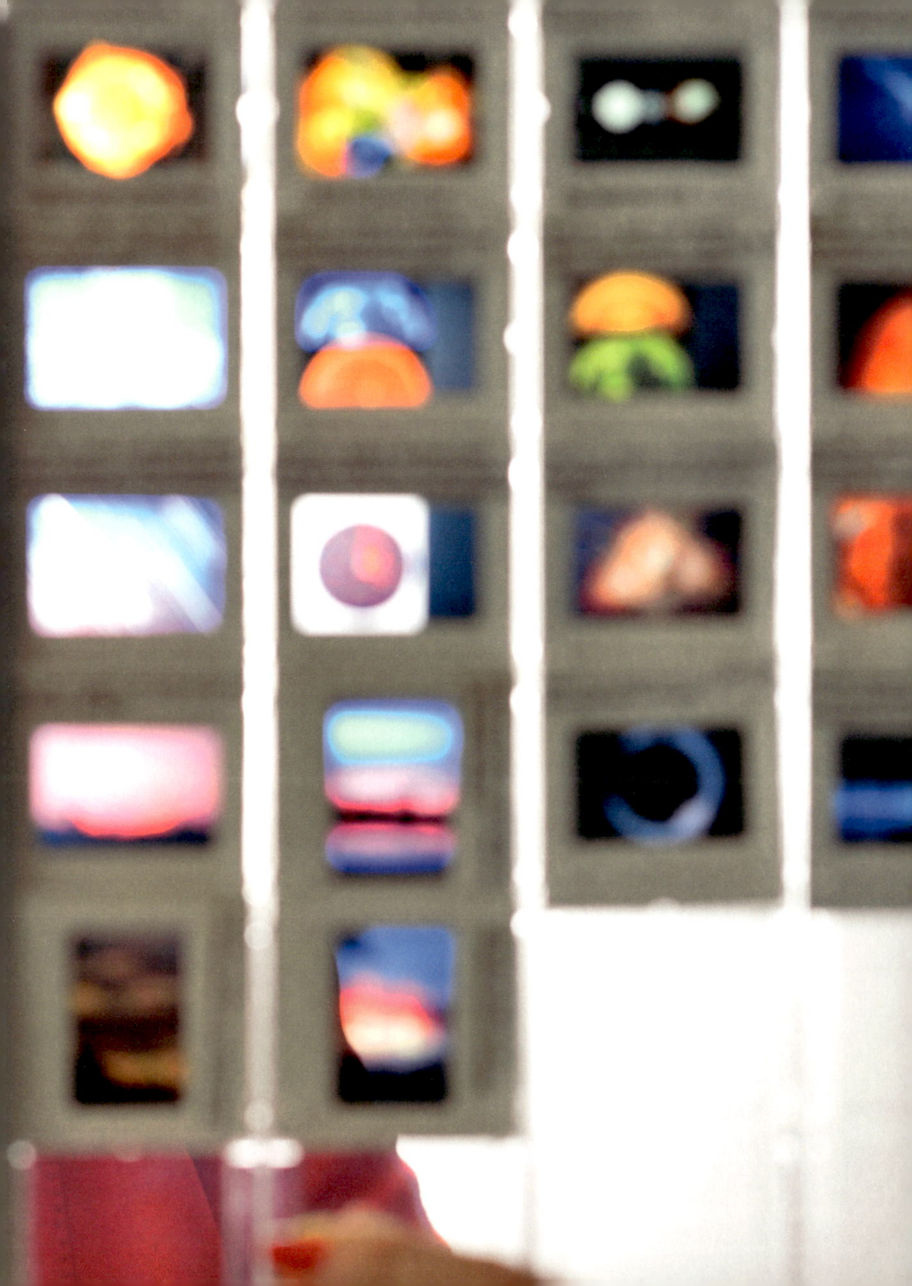

WHAT'S MODER

1 2 3

5 6 7

9 10 11

13 14 15

17 WHY IS ART 18 19

21 22 23

25 26 27

ART?

4

8

12

16

20

24

N ART?

16 WHAT'S MODERN ART?

The word "modern" basically means "new"—and yet the term "modern art" reaches far back into the twentieth century. The beginning of modern art is generally dated to the decades around World War I (1914–18). In fact, from 1905 onwards, there emerged a series of new artistic movements and styles, which have entered art history with the following names:

Fauvism (from 1905)
Expressionism (from 1905)
Cubism (from 1907)
Futurism (from 1909)
Suprematism (from 1915)
Dadaism (from 1916)
Constructivism (from 1917)
De Stijl (from 1917)
Surrealism (from 1924)
and others.

A major achievement of this epoch was the development of "abstract," or "non-objective," art. Artists began painting pictures that had no recognizable subject matter. Sculptures that represented nothing beyond themselves were also created. In addition, various materials such as cardboard, sheet metal, wire, string, and newspaper clippings found their way into art. Innovative experiments and discoveries were made, and many habits and established traditions were questioned.

Today, the pioneering works of Henri Matisse, Pablo Picasso, Wassily Kandinsky, Paul Klee, and others fall under the heading "classical modernism." Over one hundred years ago, these paintings and sculptures were viewed as revolutionary—and now, they are modern classics.

What is new art called today? — The period beginning in the mid-sixties is often referred to as "post-modern" (meaning: after modern art), and works done today or in recent years and decades are collectively called "contemporary art." Many new approaches and concepts have been tested and proposed during this period, from Conceptual Art to Political Actions, from video installations to Street Art.

Art keeps developing, and new forms of expression reflecting the spirit of the times are continually emerging. Even though the Expressionists and Cubists produced wonderful works of art, contemporary artists can't simply repeat their achievements. What has already been invented can't be re-invented. Art can't stand still or jump back to a past epoch; it can take up past art, quote it, question it—but never simply copy it.

What is art?

"Art opens up new ways of seeing the world. — Art liberates us from being imprisoned by conventions and habits of perception and thinking. — Art liberates us from mundane functioning in our day-to-day life."

Bice Curiger, curator, Kunsthaus Zürich

Bice Curiger behind Rebecca Warren's sculpture *Dark Passage,* 2004, Kunsthaus Zürich

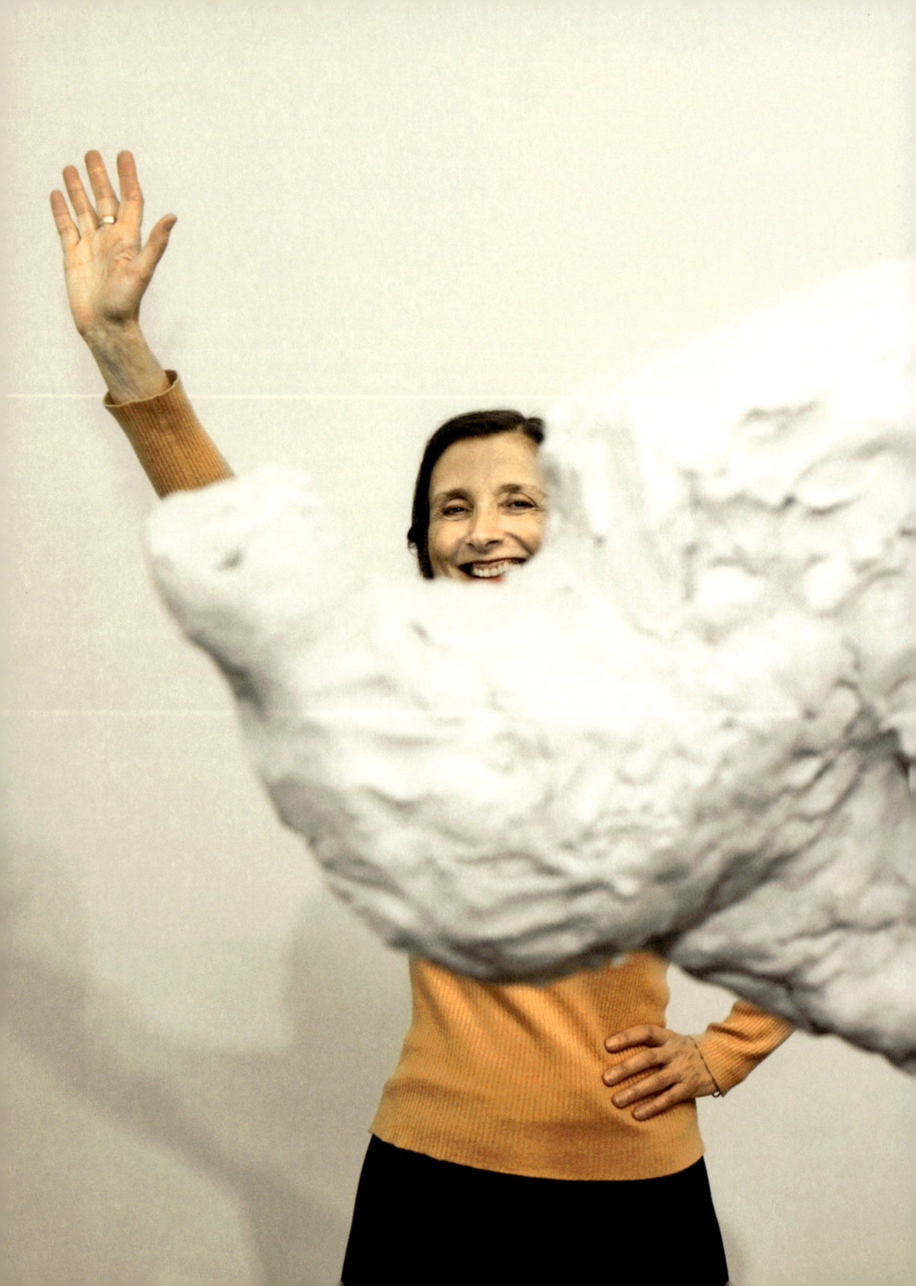

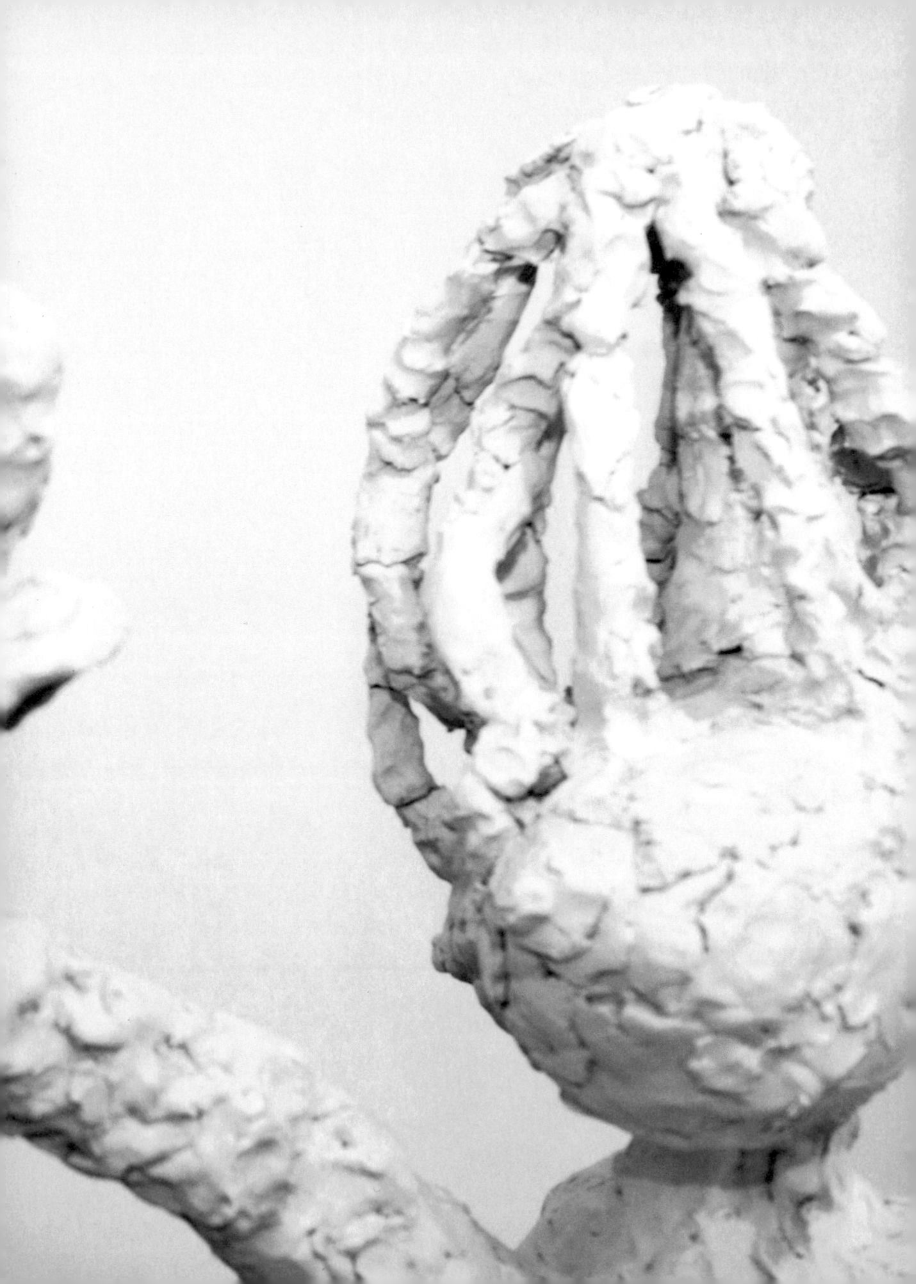

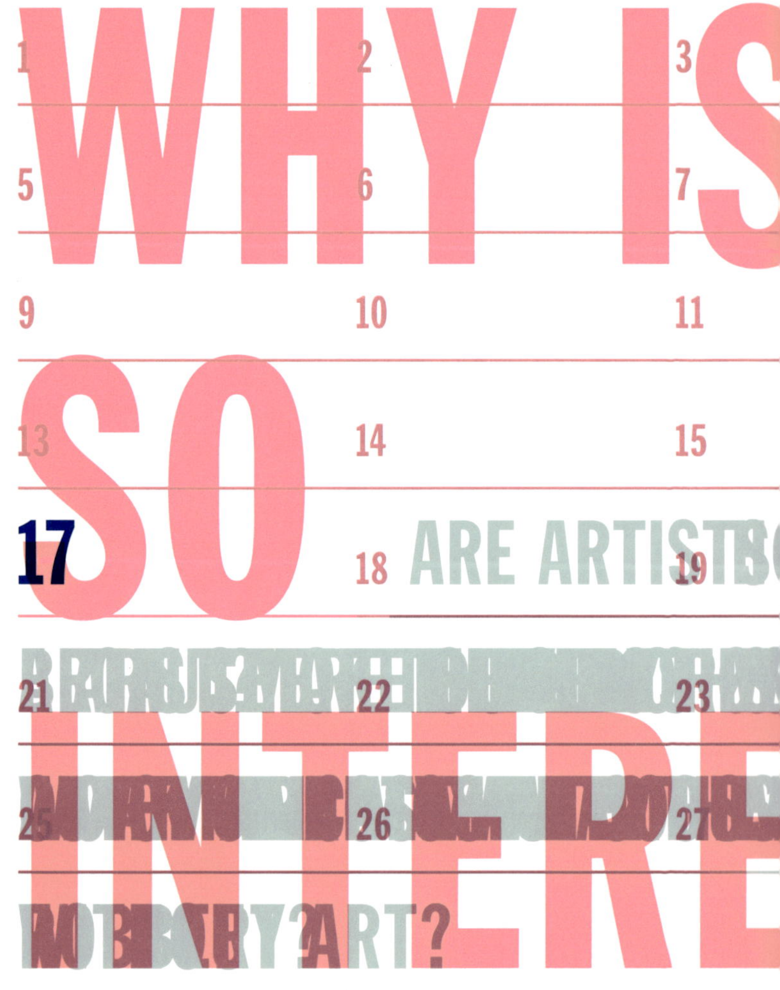
WHY IS
SO
INTERE
ARE ARTIST
ART?
1 2 3
5 6 7
9 10 11
13 14 15
17 18 19
21 22 23
25 26 27

ART

STING?

17 WHY IS ART SO INTERESTING?

- ☐ Because you can travel into the past with it.
- ☐ Because it's inspiring.
- ☐ Because it broadens your horizons.
- ☐ Because every work of art is one of a kind.
- ☐ Because there are so many marvelous works of art.
- ☐ Because it shows you something you've never seen before
- ☐ Because it speaks to the heart.
- ☐ Because it comes out of the blue.
- ☐ Because it embodies yearnings, dreams, ideals, and the meaning of life.
- ☐ Because it angers and provokes.
- ☐ Because it shows what might be.

What is art?

“Art makes visible what we feel, think, fear, or desire. — Art is when a person succeeds in creating something visible that expresses something so unusual and moving about the world and life, love, and suffering that others feel it to be true or beautiful.”

Sam Keller, Museum Director, Fondation Beyeler, Riehen/Basel

Sam Keller with Jeff Koons’s sculpture *Tulips,* 1995–98, Fondation Beyeler, Riehen/Basel

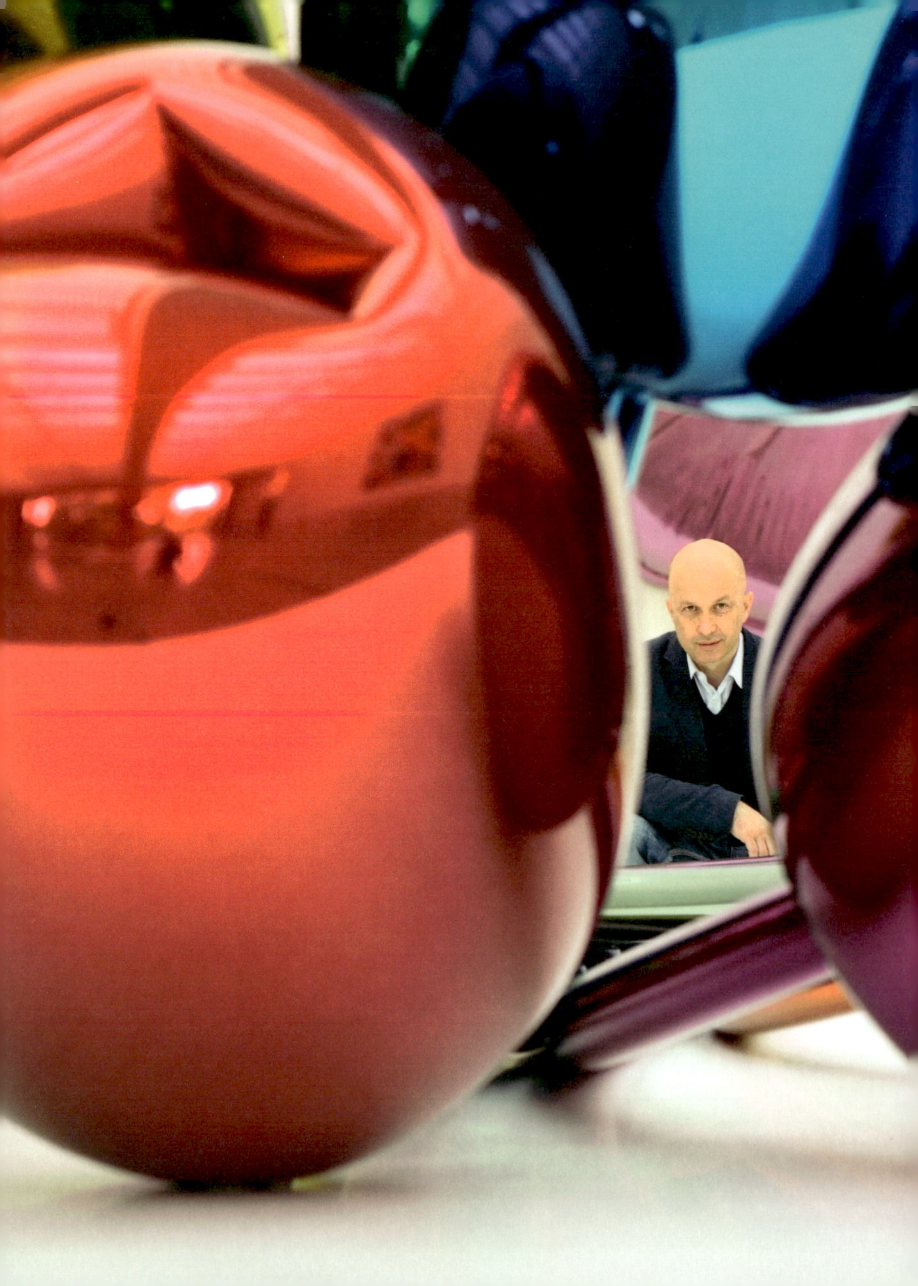

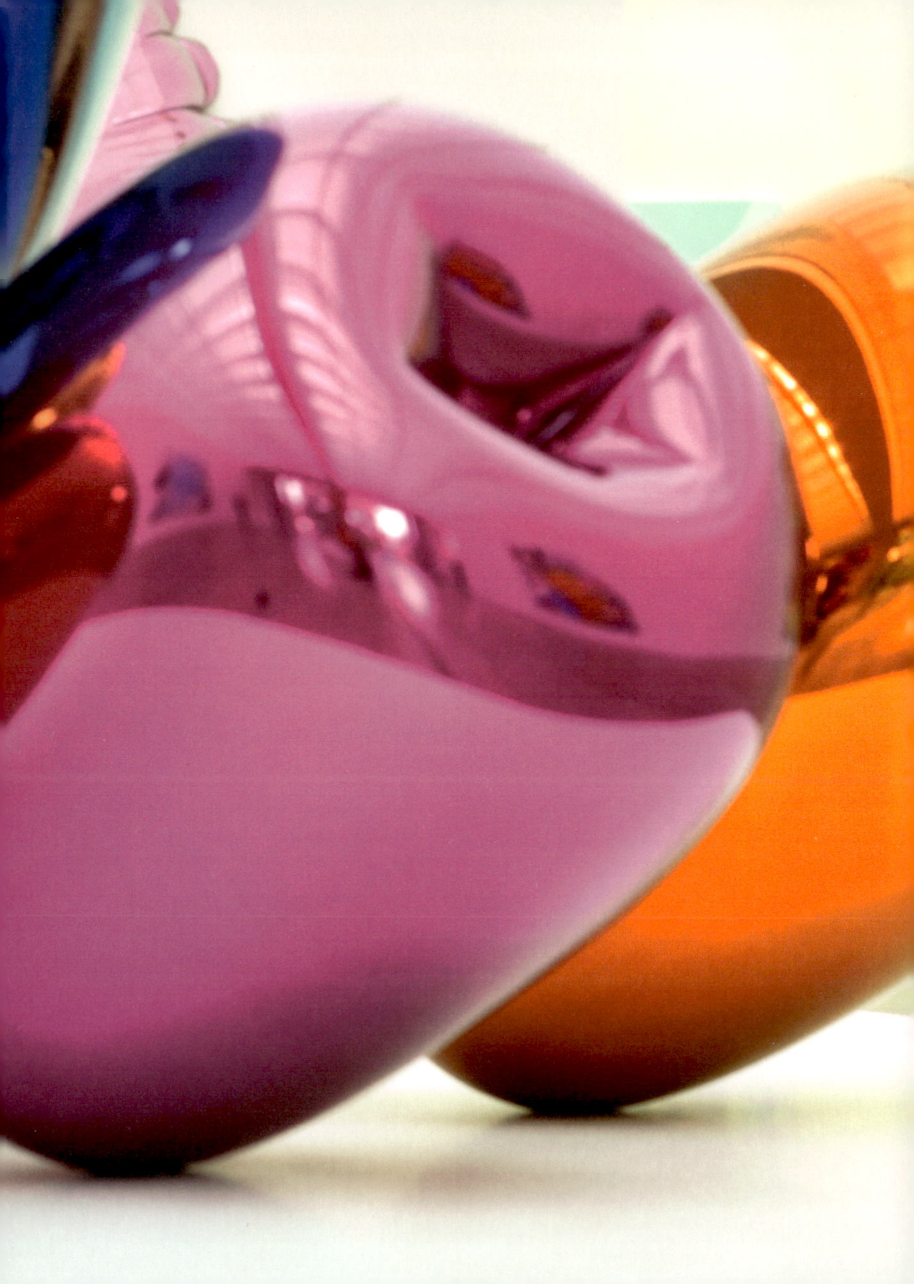

ARE ARTIS

SOMETIME

BECAUSE

18

OF THEIR W

4

8

PUNISHED

12

16

20

24

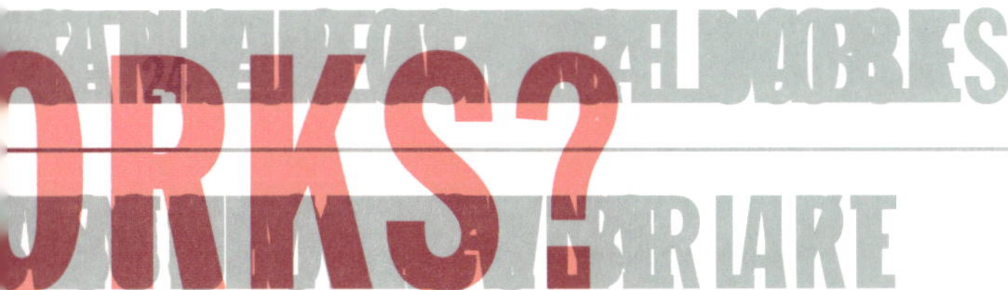

ORKS?

18 ARE ARTISTS SOMETIMES PUNISHED BECAUSE OF THEIR WORKS?

Art has the power to excite people, inspire and rouse them, provide food for thought, but also to provoke and insult them. Every era and society decides anew what is considered beautiful and ugly, good or insufferable, and where the limits of the acceptable lie. As a result, time and again throughout history, certain works of art have been confiscated, censored, or destroyed, and artists have been held accountable for their works.

In late fifteenth-century Florence, for example, the Dominican monk and hellfire-and-brimstone preacher Girolamo Savonarola ordered numerous works of art that did not conform to his teachings to be burned. He believed that art no longer served the worship of God, and that artists used religious motifs as an excuse to depict worldly pleasures and naked bodies.

In the twentieth century, the Nazis had their own particular ideas about what sort of art was "correct," and denounced anything that did not fit their definition as being "degenerate." About 16,000 works of Expressionist, Dada, New Objectivity, Surrealist, Cubist, and Fauvist art were removed from German museums. Many of the artists affected were forbidden not only to exhibit but also to work at all. Art professors, such as the painter Paul Klee, lost their teaching posts, and many fled to the U.S.

A more recent case took place in 2011 in China. Ai Weiwei, a conceptual artist, sculptor, and curator famous for his political works of art, was imprisoned on April 3, 2011—supposedly because he avoided paying taxes—and not released until months later, on June 22, on bail and under strict conditions. The Chinese foreign ministry spokesman explained that "provocative people like Ai Weiwei must be kept in check."

Ai Weiwei holding part of his 167-piece sculpture *Mei Le* and standing next to two casts of his sculpture *Marble Arm,* both 2007, in his Beijing studio

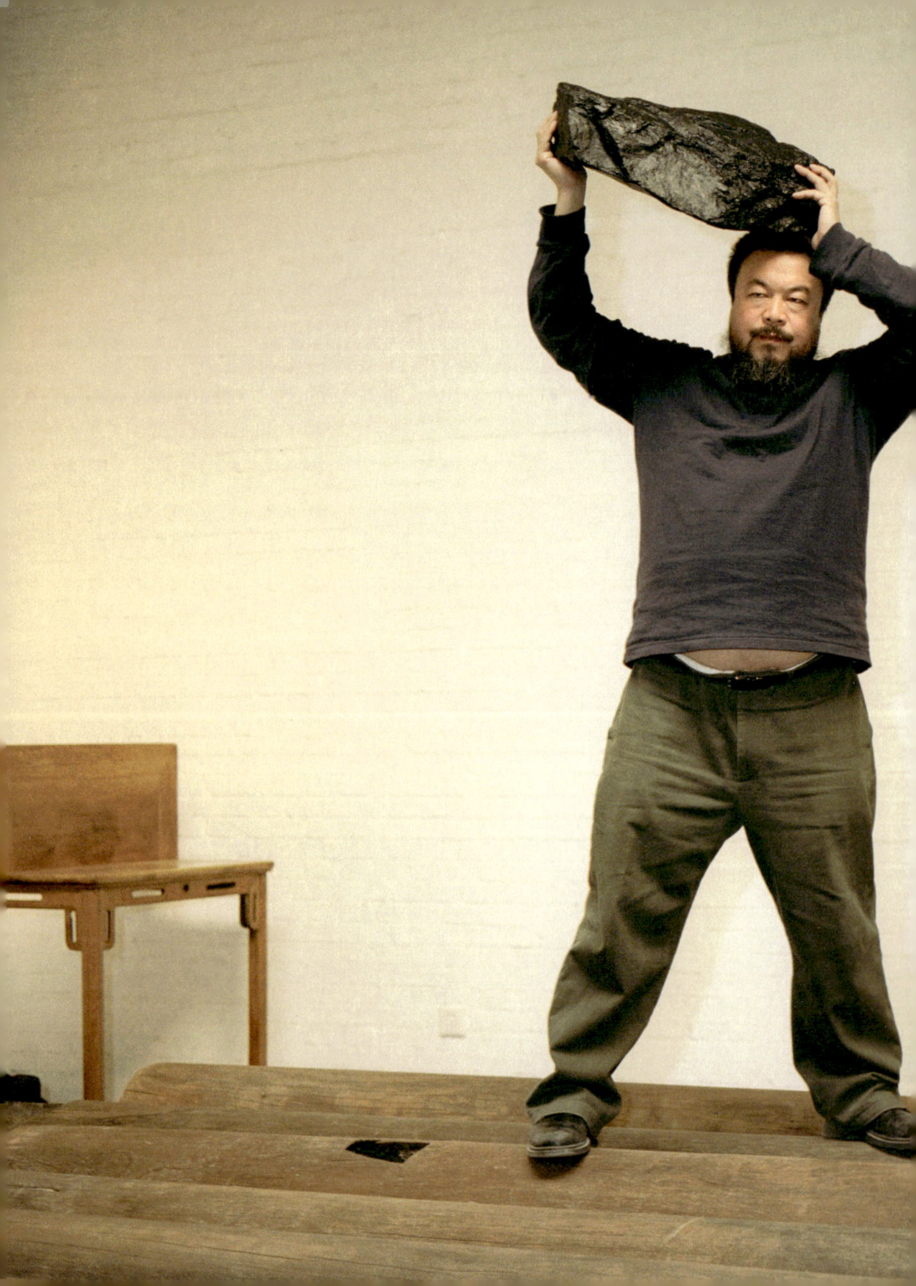

HOW MANY
CAN AN AR
MAKE DUR
HER LIFET

1 2 3
5 6 7
9 10 11
13 14 15
17 18 **19**
21 22 23
25 26 27

ART?

ARTWORKS

4

8

IST

12

16

G HIS OR

20 CAN ANYONE BE AN

24

E?

19 HOW MANY ARTWORKS CAN AN ARTIST MAKE DURING HIS OR HER LIFETIME?

The French painter Claude Monet created 1,983 oil paintings during his lifetime, Paul Cézanne 954, Henri Rousseau 261, Edvard Munch 1,789, René Magritte 1,094, Wassily Kandinsky 1,177, Paula Modersohn-Becker 734, Joan Miró 2,078, and the American artist Georgia O'Keeffe 821.

If we want to know just how many works an artist made, we turn to the list of complete works known as a catalogue raisonné. Ideally, this catalogue also illustrates every work, and gives the title, medium (material), technique, dimensions, date, current location, and origin. The total number of works created depends on a number of factors, such as the artist's biographical situation, working methods, materials used—and simply on time, that is, the artist's lifetime as well as the circumstances of the times in which he or she lived.

Often, only very few works by artists who lived in earlier periods have survived. We can't know how many they actually created because many works were lost due to negligence or low valuation, or were destroyed during periods of war.

One artist who recorded his life's work was the German painter Paul Klee. From February 1911 to his death in 1940, Klee kept a handwritten list of all his works. He even had a copy made of the first volume in 1916, fearing he might lose his own during the war. Klee's catalogue raisonné is a very valuable document. Only rarely has an artist so carefully and comprehensively recorded his own works:

	733	paintings
	4,877	drawings
	3,197	colored works on paper
	54	etchings
	38	lithographs
	3	woodcuts
	16	sculptures
Total:	**8,918**	**works**

What is art?

"When somebody sees something special and makes something special out of it; when this person makes this special thing visible for others; when they see what is special about it for the artist: that is art. — Art expands and sharpens our own perception, both when making and when viewing it. It puts us in a raised state of awareness and gives us food for thought."

Monica Studer and Christoph van den Berg, artists, Basel

Monica Studer and Christoph van den Berg with their installation
A Band of Floating Mushrooms, 2011, Kunstfreilager Dreispitz, Basel

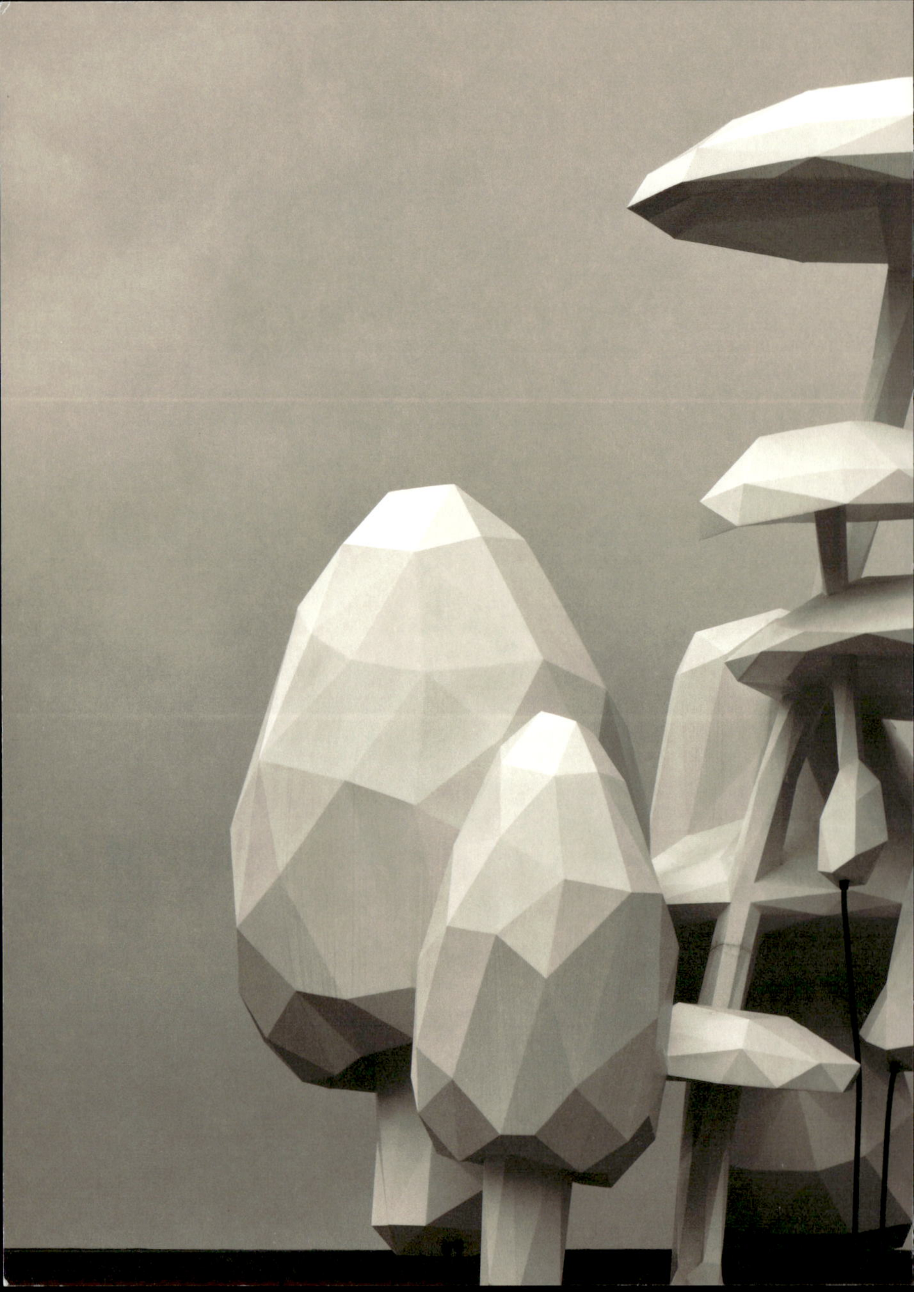

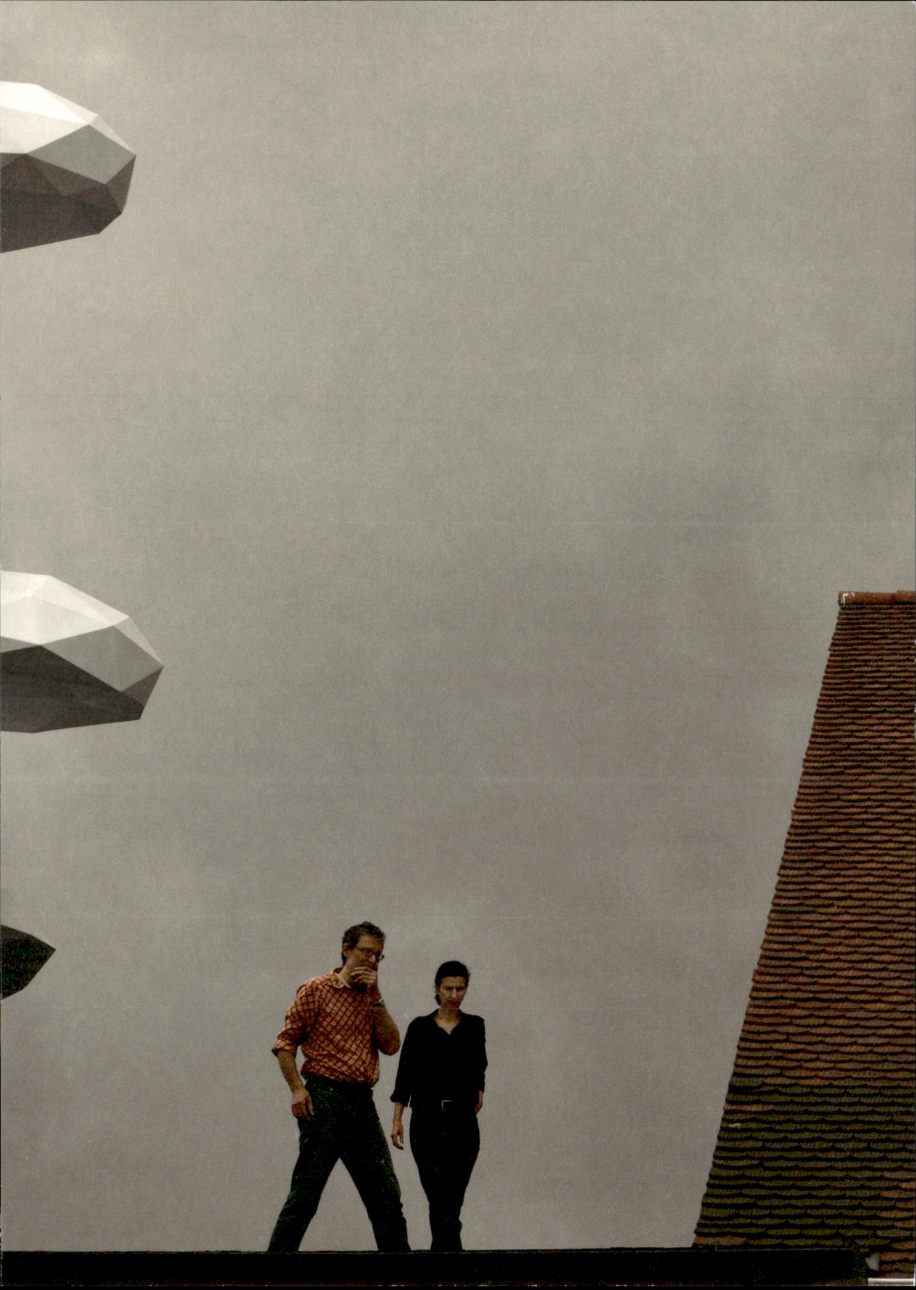

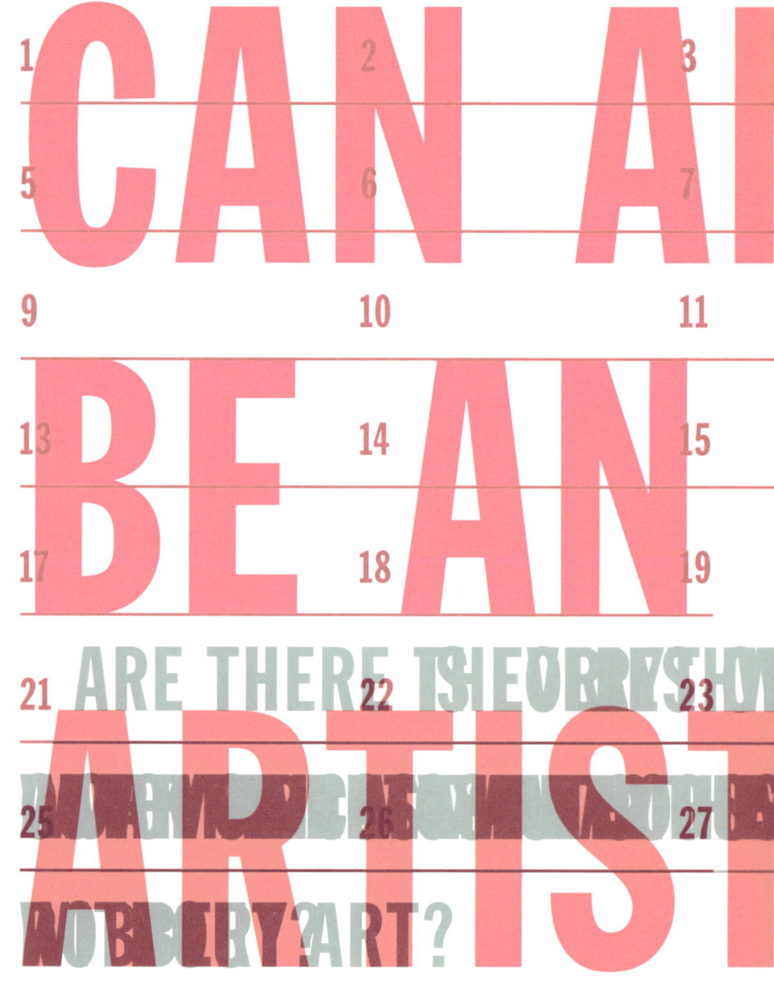

CAN A
BE AN
ARTIST
ARE THERE
ART?
1 2 3
5 6 7
9 10 11
13 14 15
17 18 19
21 22 23
25 26 27

YONE

4

8

12

16

20

24

S

R LA RE

20 CAN ANYONE BE AN ARTIST?

The German artist Joseph Beuys believed anyone can. As a professor at the Düsseldorf Kunstakademie, in addition to his regular students, in 1971–72, he admitted all the applicants who had been rejected by the other professors into his class. This, of course, went against regulations, and led to a long legal dispute between Beuys and the academy.

In past centuries, only those who had proper training could become artists. Women were excluded from academy attendance, which explains why there were very few female artists. Professors of art determined who was allowed to study the subject and how art was to look. In addition, they sat on the juries of the great national exhibitions. In France, these were known from the seventeenth century onwards as the Salon, which took place in Paris. Participation was a must to achieve public recognition and financial success. The strict jury regularly rejected numerous applicants.

In the middle of the nineteenth century, rejected artists began to hit back. First, they established the Salon des Refusés (Salon of Rejected Artists), then the Salon des Indépendants (Salon of Independent Artists), a non-juried show in which anyone could present his or her works—even Henri Rousseau, who had taught himself how to paint.

Nowadays, anyone can call themselves an "artist" because this is not a protected professional title like "architect" or "doctor." Whether this name is accepted by the art scene is another matter, however. People who have not attended art college are often dismissed as "Sunday painters" or "hobby artists," even today.

In order to find recognition in the art world, not only good ideas and creativity are needed but incredible willpower. Artists must continually battle with barriers and defend their work against doubters, as well as their own self-doubt. This is easier when you have the opportunity to study at an art college. This is not only a place where you acquire skills but also learn about ideas and theories, and have a chance to exchange views about your work with like-minded people.

Visitors next to David Shrigley's installation *I'm Dead,* 2010, at the Stephen Friedman Gallery booth, Frieze Art Fair, London, 2010

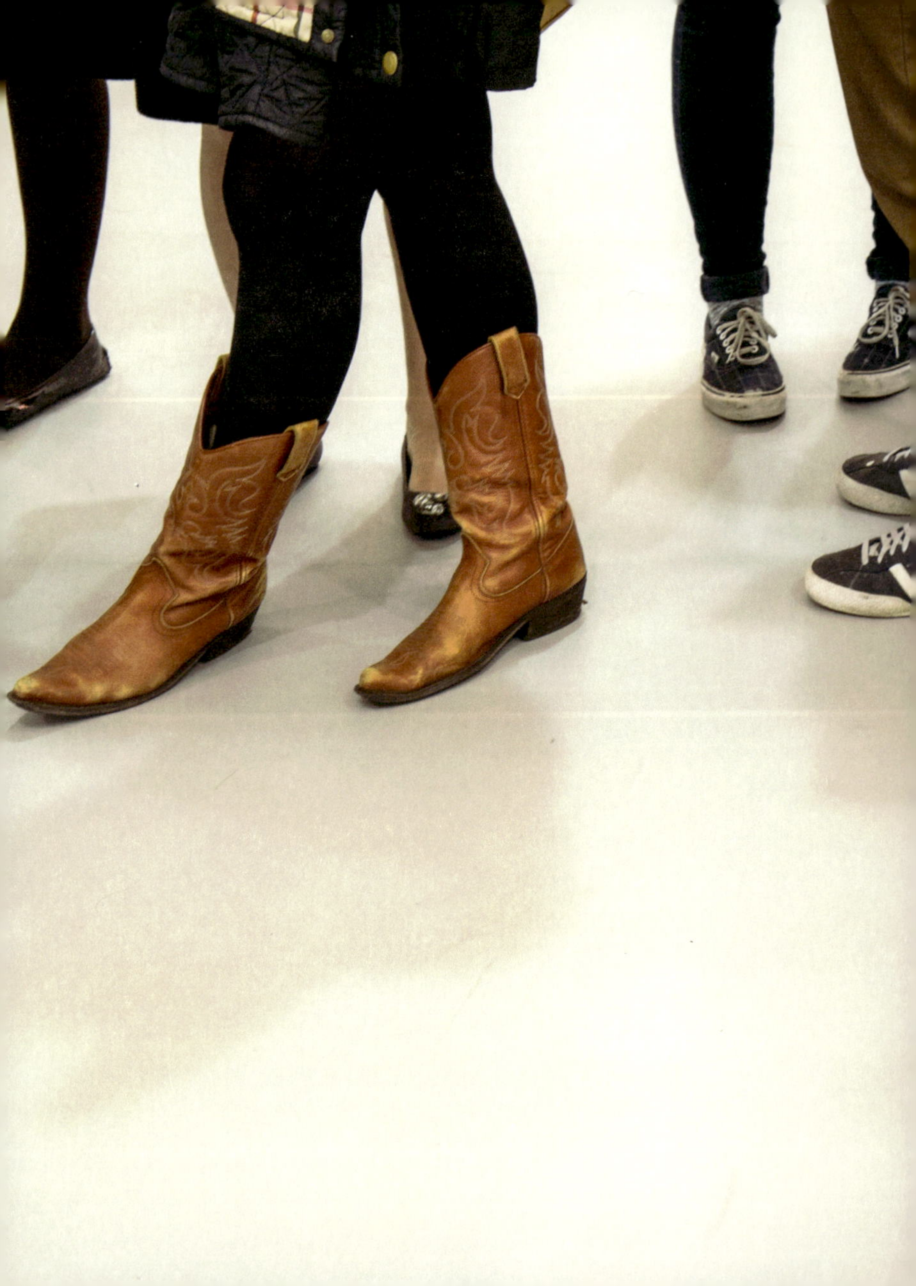

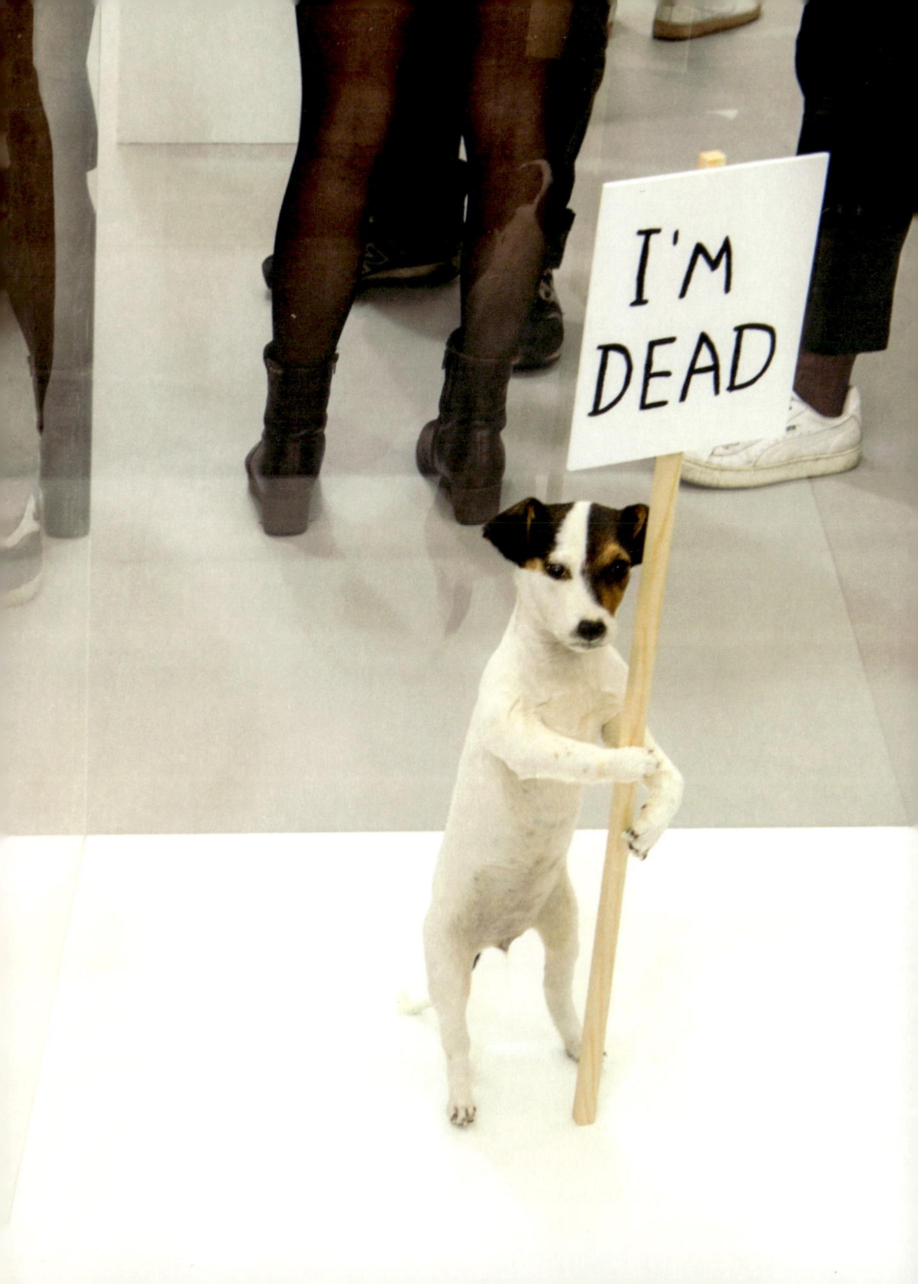
I'M
DEAD

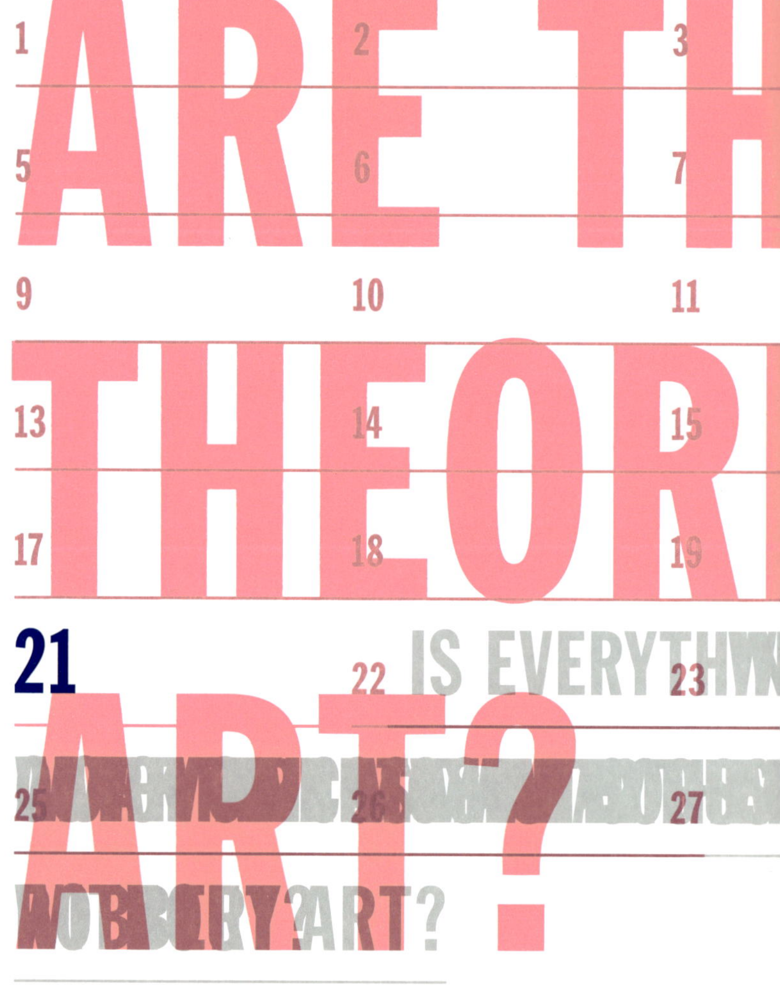
ARE TH
THEORI
ART?
IS EVERYTH
ART?
1
2
3
5
6
7
9
10
11
13
14
15
17
18
19
21
22
23
25
26
27

ERE

4

8

12

ES OF

16

20

24

21 ARE THERE THEORIES OF ART?

People concerned with art continually put forward new theories about it and reject them again. Everyone wants to explain how art affects us and what it means. A work of art is never produced in a vacuum, but always at a particular point in time and in a certain place. There are no artists who "simply make" something. If we look more closely, this "simply" always turns out to have many layers and to be complex. Sometimes, theoretical considerations rush ahead of art; other times, they lag behind. And it's not uncommon for artists themselves to make a point of commenting on their works, explaining them in writing, or "justifying" them in terms of some theory. Often, artists join groups in order to state their common aims and convictions.

First theory, then art — The group of French painters around Georges Seurat and Paul Signac came to be called "Post-Impressionists." Their aim was to develop a scientifically founded style out of Impressionism. They were also called "Divisionists" because they didn't mix colors but "divided" them into pure dots of color. Or, they were termed "Pointillists" because of the countless points, or dots, of which their pictures consisted. They based their works on scientific studies, especially the insights of the French chemist Michel-Eugène Chevreul, who, in the nineteenth century, examined the luminosity and contrasting effects of colors.

First art, then theory — From 1908 to 1913, Pablo Picasso and Georges Braque developed a manner of painting that went down in art history as "Cubism," a name that poked fun at the style. Their pictures were so revolutionary, puzzling, and shocking that they sparked heated debates not only in Paris but in many European cities. Soon, the first theories of Cubist painting emerged. These were written mainly by authors, art critics, and fellow artists. A book still highly regarded today—*The Path to Cubism,* 1920—was written by Daniel-Henry Kahnweiler, Picasso's dealer at the time.

Art and theory are inseparable — In Surrealism, one of the most significant movements in the twentieth century, art and theory were closely related. The artists were at the same time theoreticians. In 1924, André Breton published the *Manifesto of Surrealism,* in which he defined the group's aims and which was signed by many of his artist friends. The Surrealists set out to find the true sources of creativity and demanded absolute freedom of thought and artistic creation. They were in favor of relying on dreams, uncontrolled actions, delusions, and repressed or hidden desires. Many other Surrealist artists, such as Max Ernst and René Magritte, never tired of writing theoretical texts alongside their work in painting.

What is art?

**"A B C D E F G H I J K L M N O P Q R S T U V W X Y Z , „ : ? ! .
S, M, L, XL
Bildergedächtnis Gedächtnisbilder
Daily Mirror Book
Zeitung
Sehen Sehen
Cats, Cats, Cats
Learning from Las Vegas
Learning from Martigny
History
Politics
Postproduction
Curating Subjects
Selected Standards
Figures of Speech
Reprocessing Reality
The Possibility of the Impossible
Minor Histories: Statements, Conversations, Proposals
Mappa
Everybody's Autobiography
Time Action Vision
Liquid Life
Heterotopias
Undoing Gender
Black Noise
Venus in Furs
The No Texts
Some Scenic Views
The Idea of the West
1983, 1984–86, 1987–90, 1991
Trajectories and Destinations
Land Route
On Boundaries
On Super-Diversity
Glamorama
Infotainment
The Meaning of Flowers
Atlas Mnemosyne
Lapdogs of the Bourgeoisie
Vivre libre ou mourir
Next Flag
High Price, Between the Market and Celebrity Culture
Pop or Populus
Theft is vision
Je mange un œuf
Ideology Reloaded
Sculpture Musicale"**

Elodie Pong, artist, Zurich and New York

Elodie Pong in her video projection *Ersatz*, 2011, in her Zurich studio

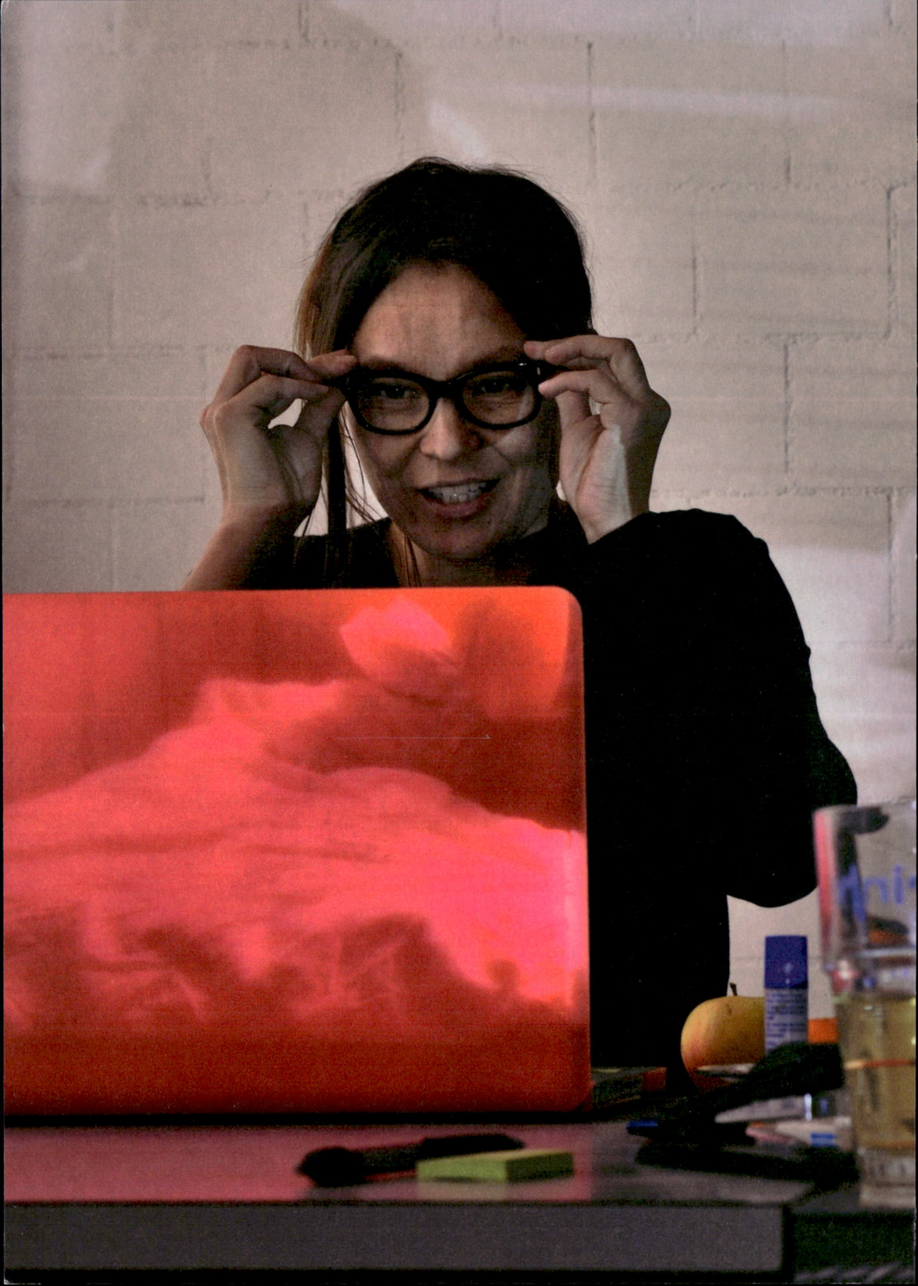

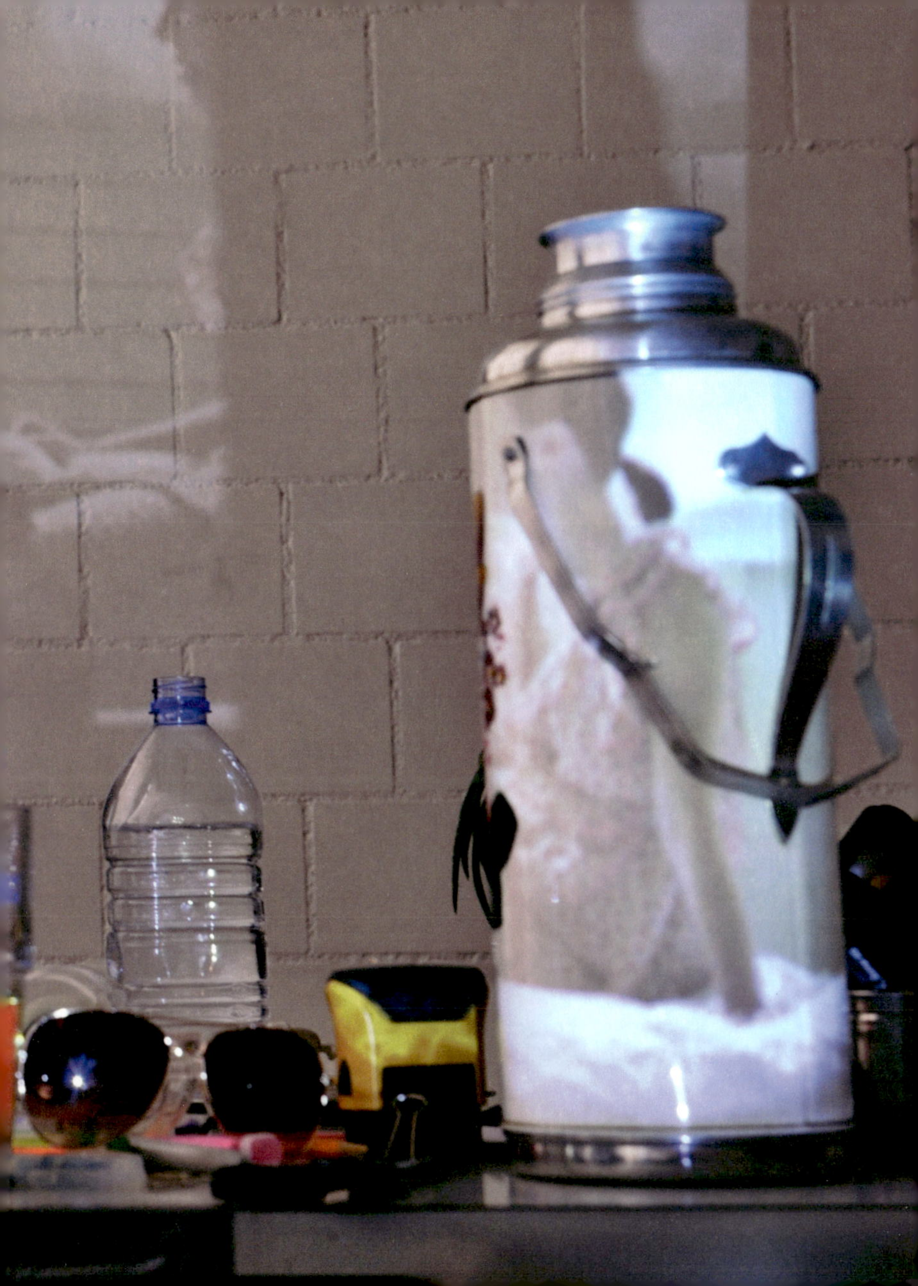

IS EVERYTH

A FAMOUS

DOES

AUTOMATIC

22

...ART?

NG

RTIST

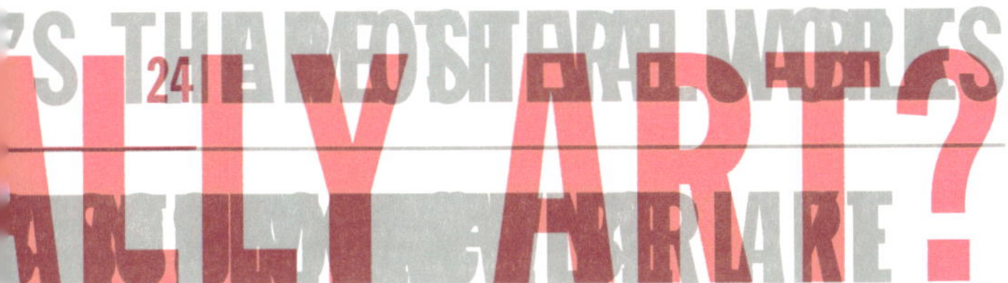

22 IS EVERYTHING A FAMOUS ARTIST DOES AUTOMATICALLY ART?

Nothing is automatically art. Artists reject many things they do because they don't think they are good enough. Take the American painter Barnett Newman. During World War II (1939–45), he became convinced that realistic, objective painting was a thing of the past. He destroyed all the paintings he had done to that point and began again from scratch.

Yet, it's not only for artists to decide whether something is art or not. Their works have to prove themselves in the art world before they can be accepted as art in the long run. The first hurdle is surely the art dealer, who must be willing to offer the works for sale. But the works do not achieve lasting status as art until they are shown in exhibitions and, ideally, included in museum collections.

The better known artists are, the more quickly their new works find acceptance. However, sometimes difficulties arise when the new works diverge stylistically too strongly from previous ones. Henri Matisse was first laughed at when, in the forties, he stopped painting and turned to making pictures of cut-out paper shapes.

Yet, once artists have attained cult status, they are treated much like other stars and there is a demand for anything they produce. This may explain, for instance, why even Leonardo da Vinci's sketches are now shown in exhibitions. In his own day, they never would have been viewed as independent works of art.

Visitors in front of Kehinde Wiley's painting *Femme Piquée Par Un Serpent,* 2008, at the Sean Kelly Gallery booth, Art Basel Miami Beach, 2010

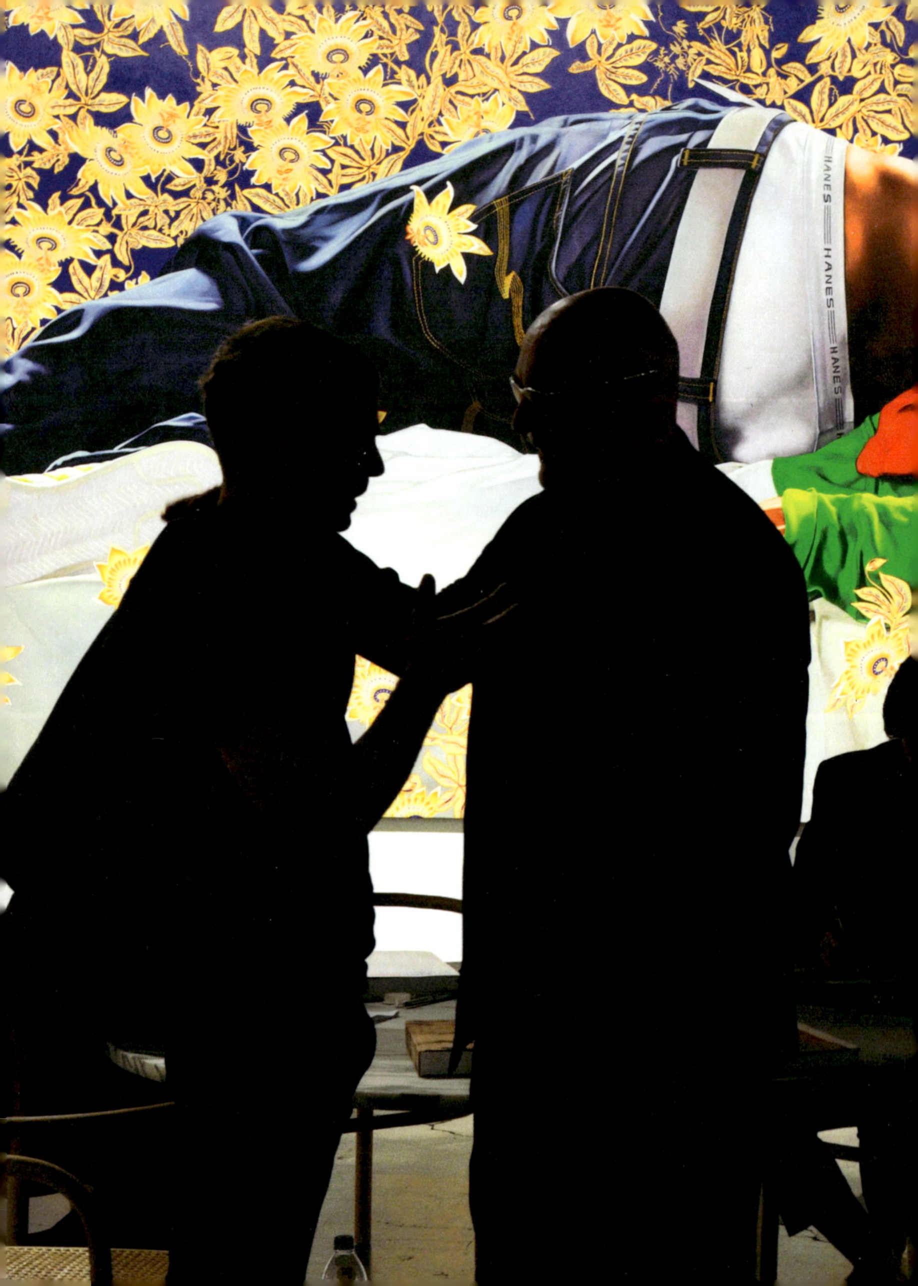
HANES
HANES
HANES
HANES

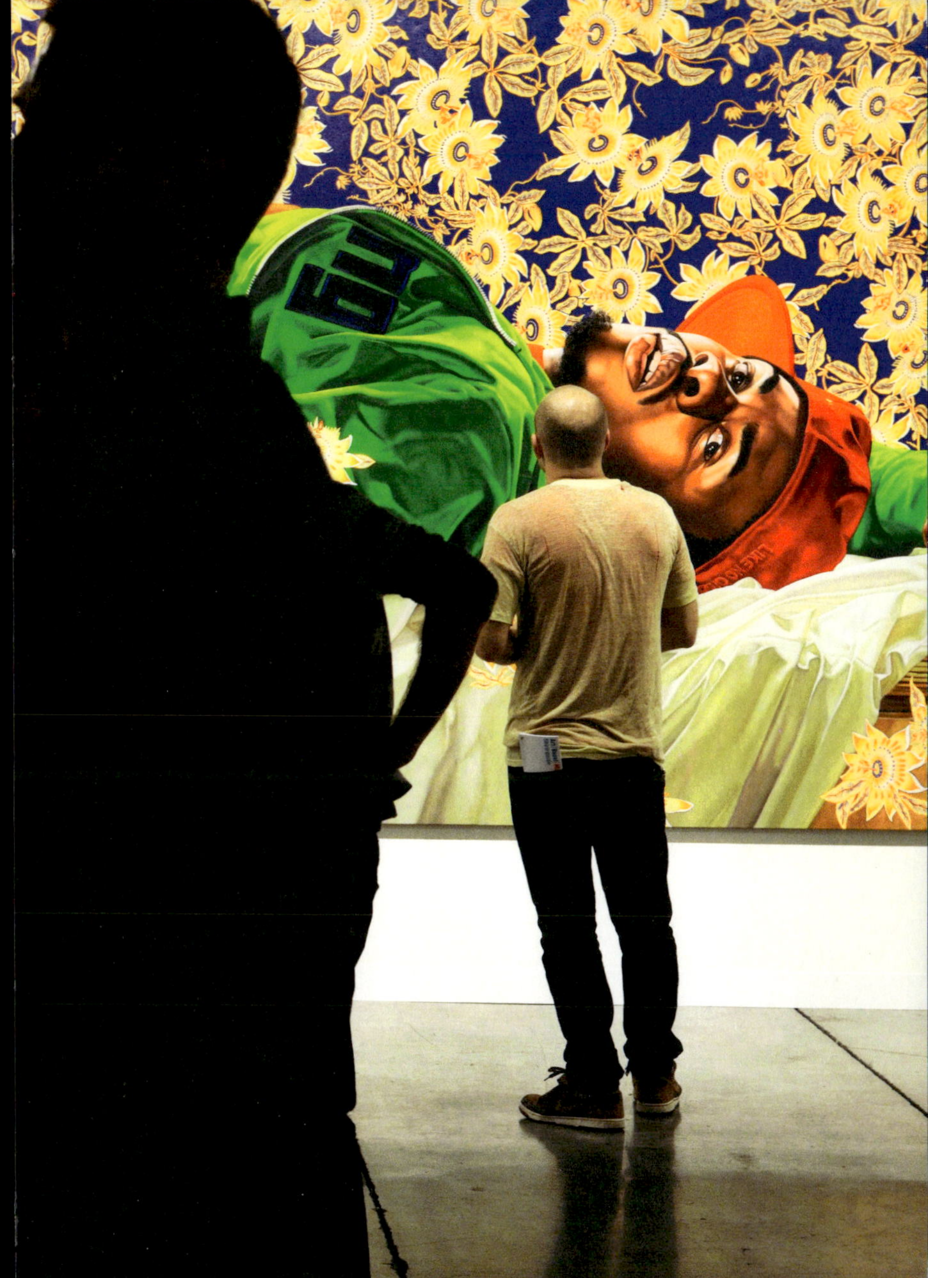

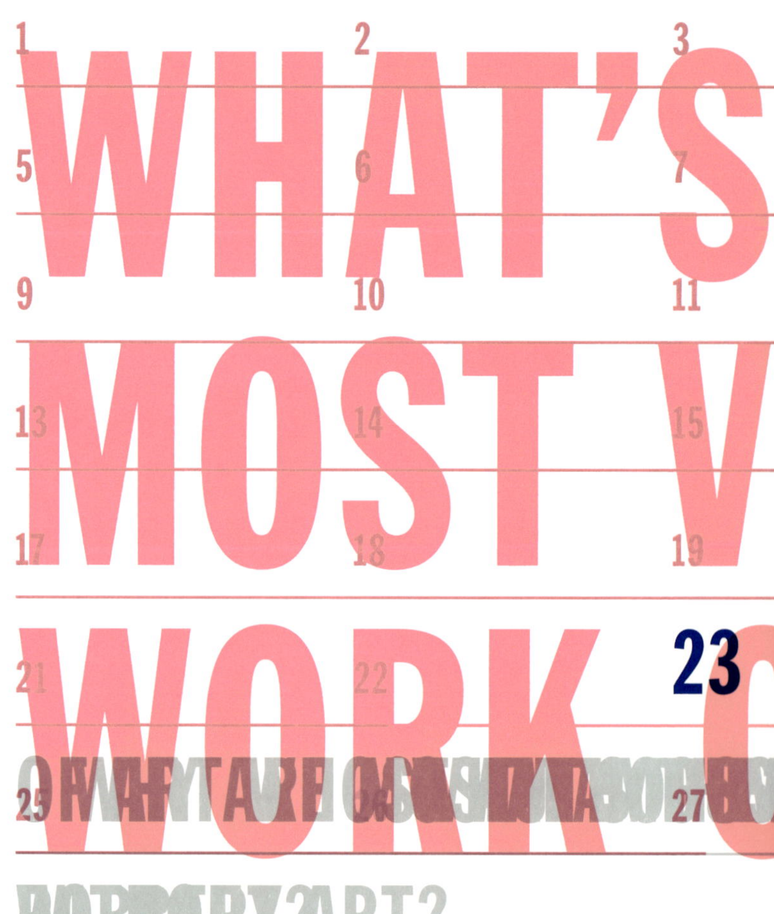
WHAT'S
MOST V
WORK O
1
2
3
5
6
7
9
10
11
13
14
15
17
18
19
21
22
23
25
26
27
ART?

THE

LUABLE

ARE THERE WORKS

ART?

23 WHAT'S THE MOST VALUABLE WORK OF ART?

Rankings of the most expensive paintings and sculptures in the world are often published in newspapers and on the Internet. If we sum up these listings, the following picture emerges:

Artist, *Title of work* (date)	**Price in millions of U.S. $***	Year
J. Pollock, *No. 5, 1948* (1948)	**140.0**	2006
W. de Kooning, *Woman III* (1953)	**137.5**	2006
G. Klimt, *Adele Bloch-Bauer I* (1907)	**135.0**	2006
E. Munch, *The Scream* (1895)	**119.9**	2012
P. Picasso, *Nude, Green Leaves and Bust* (1932)	**106.5**	2010
A. Giacometti, *Walking Man I* (1960)	**104.3**	2010
P. Picasso, *Boy with a Pipe* (1905)	**104.2**	2004
P. Picasso, *Dora Maar with Cat* (1941)	**95.2**	2006
G. Klimt, *Adele Bloch-Bauer II* (1912)	**87.9**	2006
M. Rothko, *Orange, Red, Yellow* (1961)	**86.9**	2012
F. Bacon, *Triptych, 1976* (1976)	**86.3**	2008
V. van Gogh, *Portrait of Dr. Gachet* (1890)	**82.5**	1990
C. Monet, *Water Lily Pond* (1919)	**80.5**	2008
J. Johns, *False Start* (1959)	**80.0**	2006
A. Renoir, *Ball at the Moulin de la Galette* (1876)	**78.1**	1990
P. P. Rubens, *The Massacre of the Innocents* (1609–11)	**76.7**	2002

* These prices have not been corrected for inflation.

The impressive thing about this list is not only the enormous sums paid for these works of art but the fact that some of the paintings are not even among the "major works" of the artists named. We can assume that works of art exist that are even more valuable but not for sale, for instance, Leonardo da Vinci's *Mona Lisa.* Sometimes, purchase prices are not publicly announced. Paul Cézanne's *Card Players* is said to have changed hands in spring 2011 for the record sum of 250 million dollars.

Supply and demand determine the price, as opposed to the value, of a work of art. Countless paintings and sculptures are not for sale and will never enter the art trade because they belong to museum collections, for example. The pyramids and cathedrals and other art treasures from antiquity or the Middle Ages have no price either, and yet they are of inestimable value.

What is art?

“Art is a very personal translation of observations, ideas, and feelings into a concrete shape. It expresses the nature of the artist’s personality and, at the same time, is witness to the epoch in which it was made. A work of art records the burning questions of existence facing a creative individual and reflects—not seldom in a coded way—socially urgent issues that have often not yet found entry into the public discussion at the time it was made. — Art has the effect of a catalyst that gets the attention of its viewing opposite number by means of sensory stimuli and unsettling content, and encourages a very individual involvement. The confrontation with highly expressive, moving, disturbing art is fascinating and touching; it inspires a very particular way of thinking about life in general.”

Claudia Steinfels, Art Consultant for the UBS Art Collection, UBS, Zurich

Claudia Steinfels in the stairwell of the UBS “Felsenhof” office building in Zurich

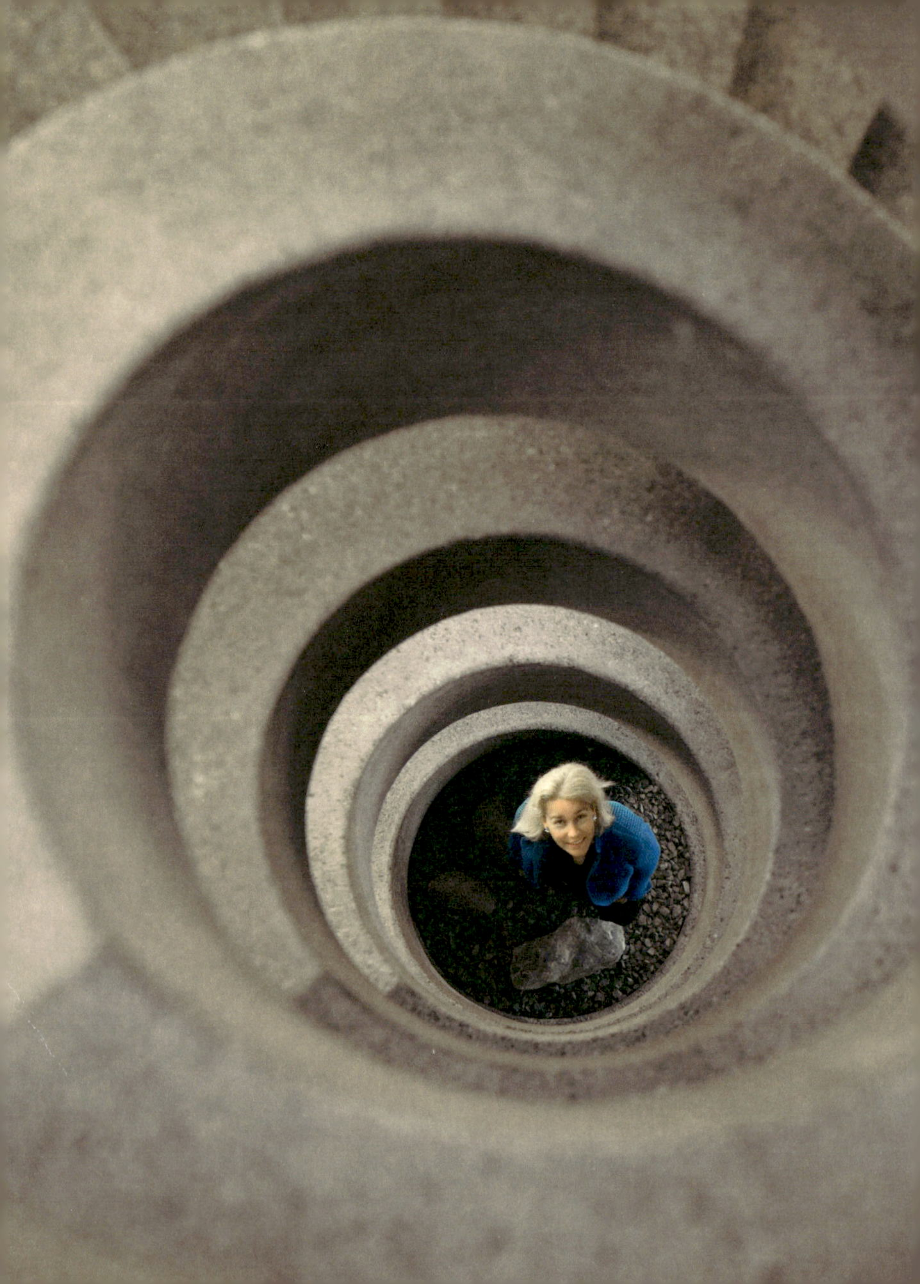

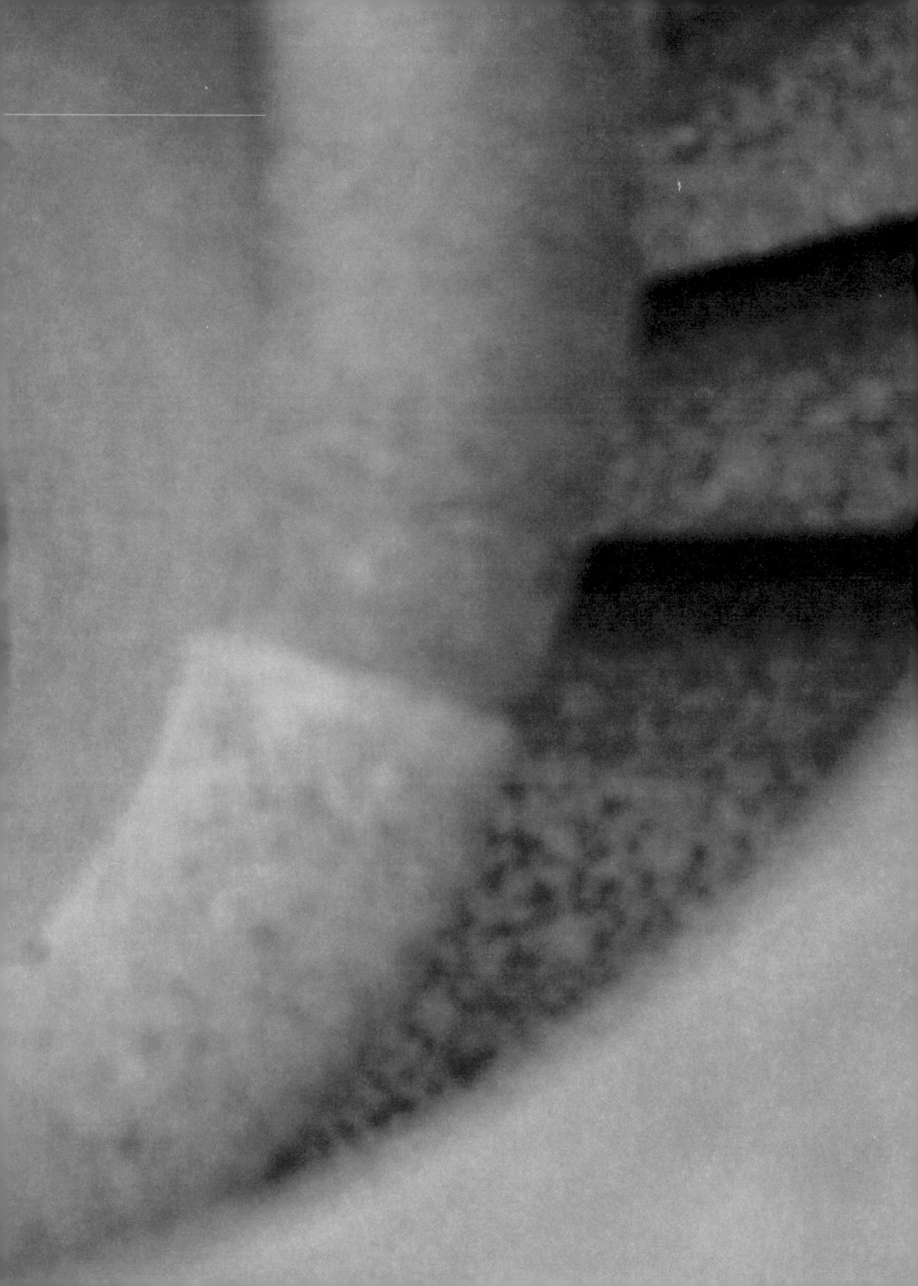

ARE THERE
OF ART WH
AUTHORS
UNKNOWN?

WHY ARE MOST

NOBODY? ART?

WORKS

4

8

SE

12

16

MAIN

20

24

24 ARE THERE WORKS OF ART WHOSE AUTHORS REMAIN UNKNOWN?

There are countless paintings, sculptures, and buildings whose makers have remained unknown, for example, from the Middle Ages. The main reason for this is that, back then, painters and sculptors in Europe had quite a different status from that of artists today. They were artisans who were responsible, say, for decorating cathedrals. Their images were intended to illustrate Bible stories as faithfully as possible, and make the all-powerfulness and works of God visible. These artisans were not expected to create anything new or brilliant. Their pictures or sculptures were not independent artworks, but part of the larger work, the church or cathedral. So, as a rule, they were not signed, and the names of their creators were not recorded for later generations.

It was not until the fifteenth century, in the Renaissance period, that the idea of the artist as a genius with innate talent was born. Now, artists came to be seen as individuals with a name and a personal artistic touch. The contents of artworks became more varied, and a picture was now thought to be "good" when it mirrored reality.

Many paintings that were once part of church altarpieces are now in museums, and we view them divorced from their original context. They confront us just as much in their own right as do modern paintings. Rather than providing the artists' names, the labels next to the pictures sometimes give makeshift names like "Master of the Colmar Crucifixion" or "Master of the Frankfurt Garden of Eden," which have been invented by art historians. As it is normal nowadays to associate a certain artistic personality with each work, an attempt is made to detect the personal touch of unknown artists, even in medieval art.

What is art?

“Art is what one sees as art. — Art keeps us company in daily life, in nature, architecture, painting, crafts, music, etc. — Art tells me stories, both past and future.”

Bertalan Bozsanyi, guard, Oskar Reinhart Collection “Am Römerholz,” Winterthur

Bertalan Bozsanyi in front of the tapestry *The Shepherd’s Life,* early sixteenth century, Oskar Reinhart Collection “Am Römerholz,” Winterthur

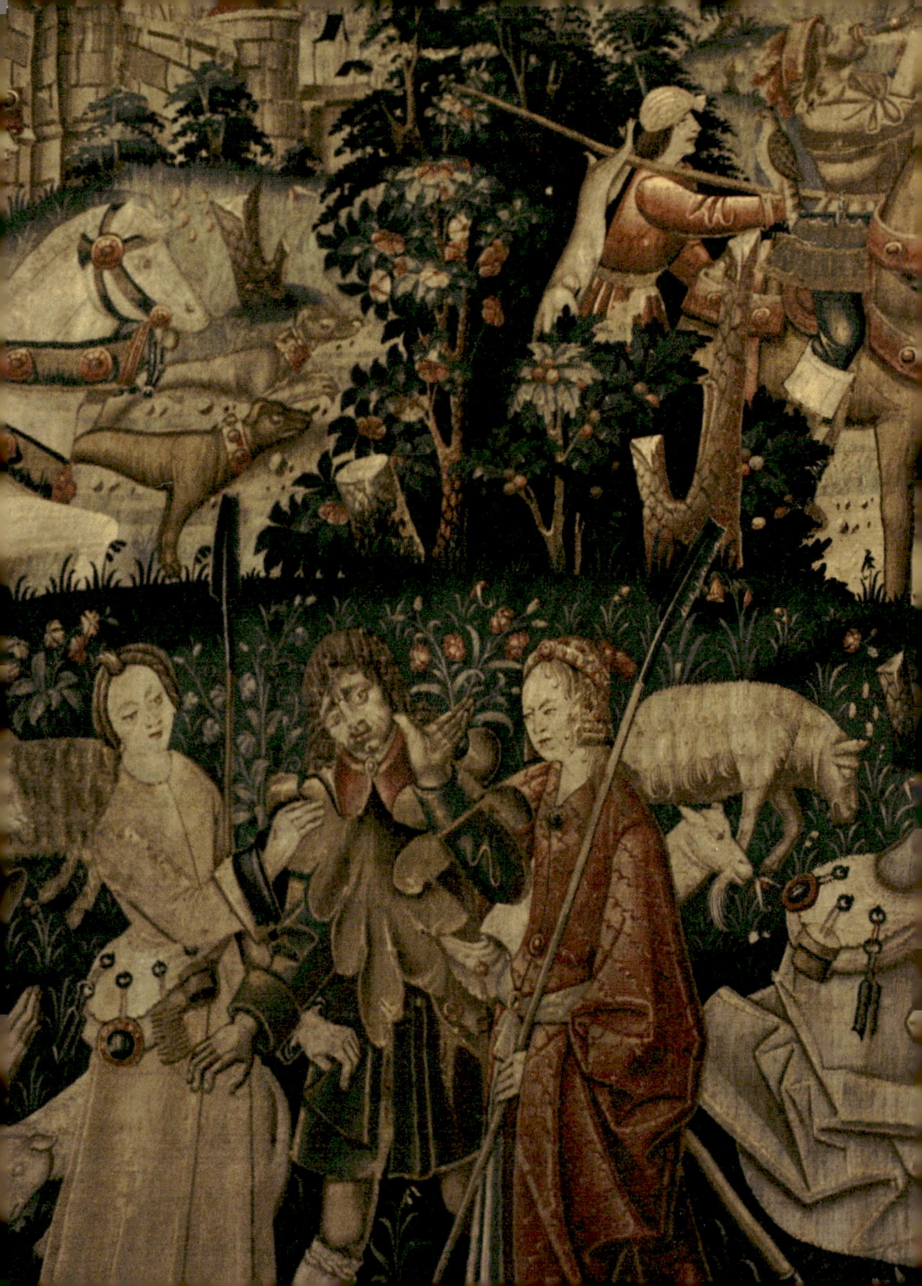

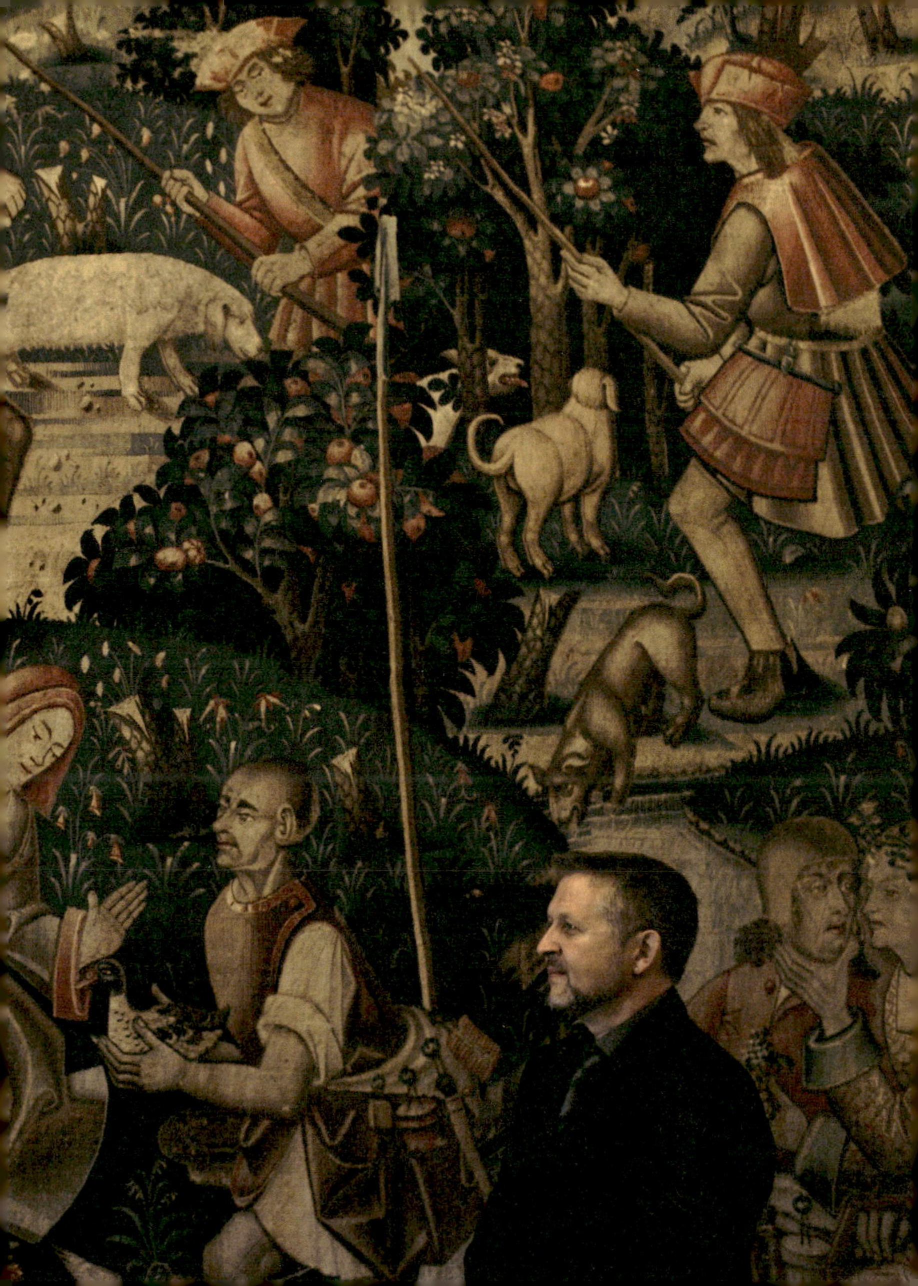

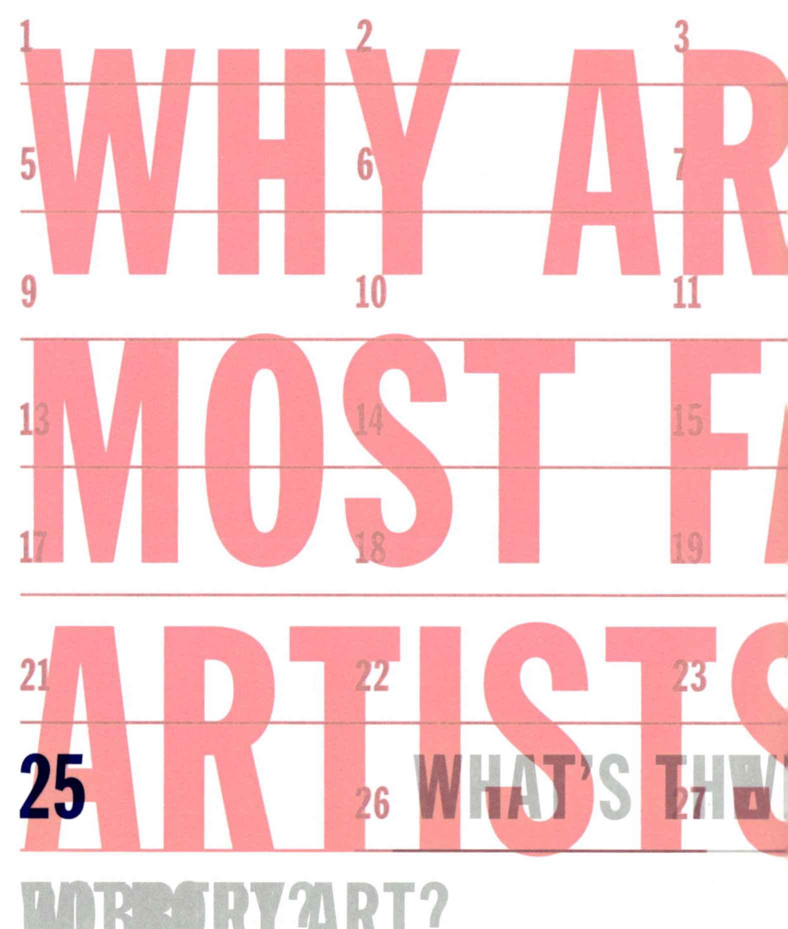
WHY AR
MOST F
ARTISTS
WHAT'S TH
1
2
3
5
6
7
9
10
11
13
14
15
17
18
19
21
22
23
25
26
27

ART?

4

8

12

MOUS

16

20

24

MEN?

25 WHY ARE MOST FAMOUS ARTISTS MEN?

This was what the Guerrilla Girls asked themselves when, wearing gorilla masks in 1985, they began to protest against the conditions reigning on the art market. Their protest was triggered by an exhibition, *An International Survey of Recent Painting and Sculpture,* at the Museum of Modern Art in New York, in which the works of 152 male artists—and only 15 female artists—were on view! After the Guerrilla Girls took stock of the largest American and European art museums, they concluded there was only one sure way for a woman to get into a museum—naked. While the proportion of female artists represented in museums was generally under five percent, over 80 percent of the nude figures in art were female.

If the museums showed only art from past centuries, this wouldn't have been so surprising because, back then, female artists were few and far between. In Leonardo da Vinci's or Rembrandt's day, power lay entirely in the hands of men. They determined which professions and occupations women were permitted to adopt. Women, they believed, were not artistically gifted by nature, so the art academies and workshops remained closed to them. A handful of female artists were successful nevertheless, and they were well known during their lifetimes. One was Artemisia Gentileschi, a Baroque painter who ran her own studio with male assistants.

Another was Angelica Kauffman, a member of two Italian academies in the eighteenth century and cofounder of the Royal Academy of Arts in London.

In the case of collections and exhibitions of modern and contemporary art, the proportion of female artists should definitely be higher. Women already began to fight for their rights in the nineteenth century, by joining art associations, studying at private academies, and, finally, managing to convince public art schools to accept female applicants. Soon, more and more women had the opportunity to become artists. Yet, the question still remains why so few of them are famous. Why were Salvador Dalí and René Magritte famous Surrealists? Why is the Surrealist Dorothea Tanning known to only a few? In order to achieve fame, women artists need to become recognized in the art world. Yet there, too, the most important positions were still held by men far into the twentieth century. Male academy professors, gallery owners, collectors, critics, curators, and museum directors still largely determined who could make a career in art, and male art historians wrote the history of art as the history of famous men.

In the meantime, female curators and art historians have begun to rewrite art history. But lots more Guerrilla Girls will be needed before just as many women as men can make a name for themselves in art!

What is art?

"Art? — My gosh! I believe that if one knew what it is, there wouldn't be any reason to do it. — Maybe because such knowledge would scare us out of doing any … or perhaps just because one of the main reasons for producing art is to find out just what art may be. — On the other hand, it's one of the few things one can get away with by asserting: it's nothing, just nothing. — Second take: it's also, conveniently, everything. — And, lastly, put in a more progressive way, I would say it's just anything. — Now, one thing it's not is harmless, even if it's more so than many other activities. — A beautiful flower remains the perfect gift to a loved one. It's also an ecological disaster. — What is art? — Possibly the space between that question and its answer."

John Armleder, artist, Geneva

John Armleder in the midst of his books in one of his art depots in Geneva

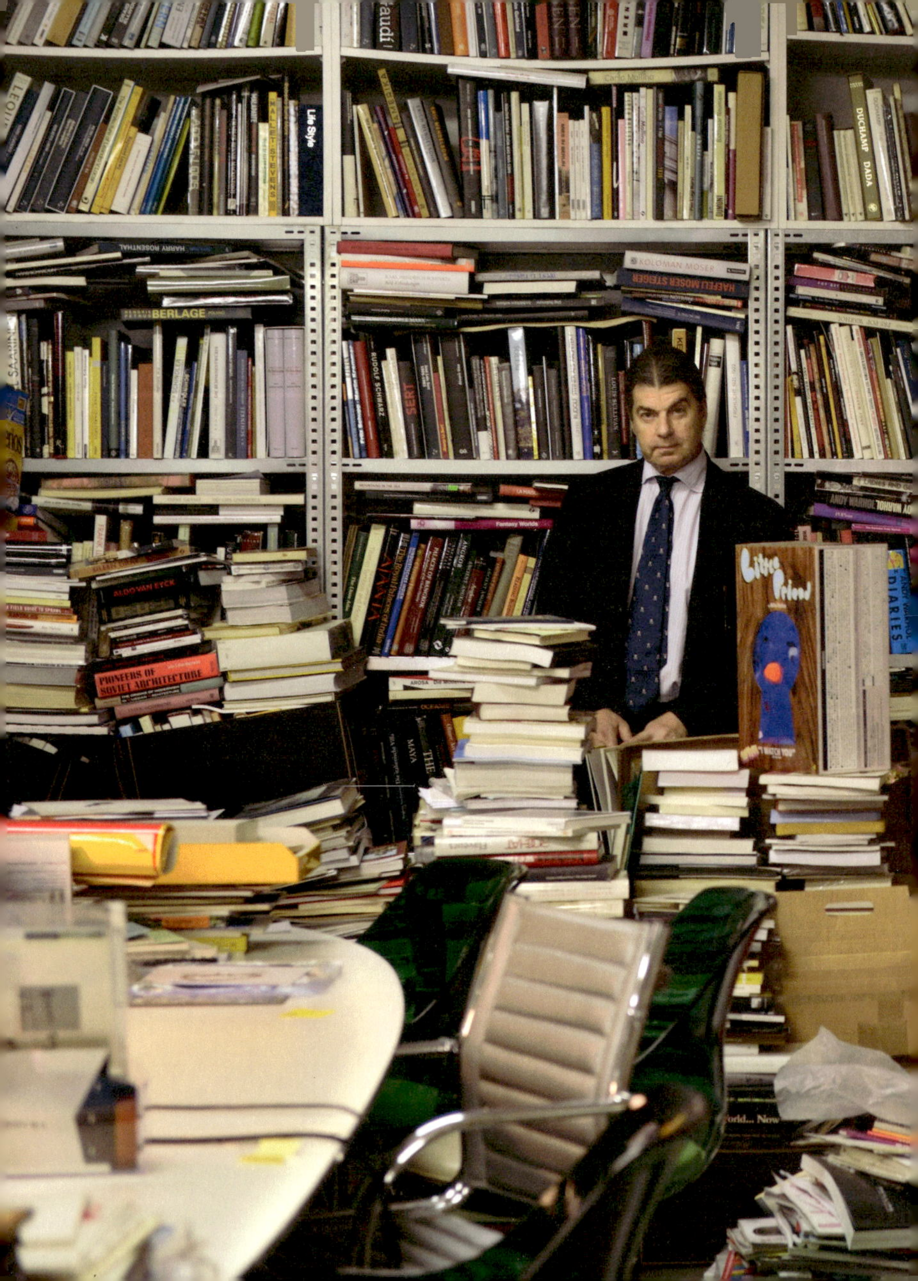
Gaudí
Carlo Mollino
Life Style
DUCHAMP
DADA
HARRY ROSENTHAL
KOLOMAN MOSER
HAEFELI MOSER STEIGER
BERLAGE
RUDOLF SCHWARZ
SERT
Fantasy Worlds
ANDY WARHOL
ALDO VAN EYCK
PIONEERS OF
SOVIET ARCHITECTURE
DIARIES
MAYA

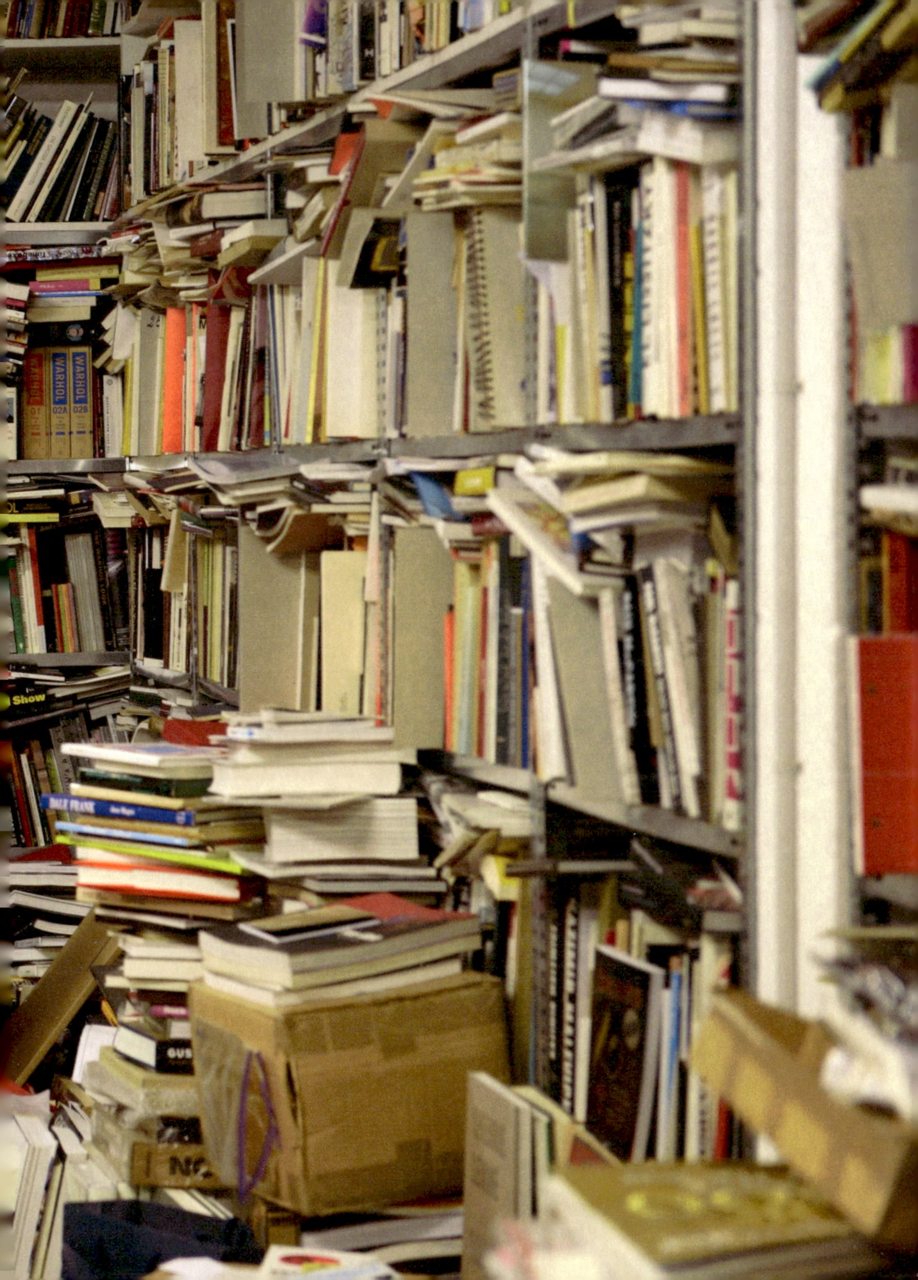
WARHOL 01
WARHOL 02A
WARHOL 02B
Show
DALE FRANK

1 2 3

WHAT'S T

5 6 7

9 10 11

SPECTAC

13 14 15

17 18 19

ART ROB

21 22 23

25 **26** 27 W

WITHOUT ART?

IE MOST
LAR
ERY?

4

8

12

16

20

24

WOULD LIFE BE LIKE

26 WHAT'S THE MOST SPECTACULAR ART ROBBERY?

On August 22, 2004, armed and masked men entered the Munch Museum in Oslo in broad daylight. They stole two major works by the Norwegian painter Edvard Munch: *The Scream* and *Madonna.* The thieves left the museum by the main entrance and fled in a waiting car. *The Scream* is one of the most famous paintings in the world, and there was hardly a chance that it could be sold anywhere on the black market. Luckily, the two pictures were secured by Norwegian police in a 2006 raid carried out in an Oslo neighborhood. Both canvases had been torn out of the frames and seriously damaged. Flaking areas of paint, moisture stains, small holes, and scratches could not be completely restored. The art thieves were arrested and sentenced to fines and several years in prison. The Munch theft was probably the most spectacular art robbery of the twenty-first century, and caused almost as much dismay as the theft of Leonardo da Vinci's *Mona Lisa* from the Louvre on August 21, 1911.

Armed robberies in museums trigger heated debate, both among the general public and among experts. How can security in exhibition spaces be improved? How can works of art be properly presented while being adequately protected? Should valuable objects of art be shown in public at all, or are they better kept in a safe? After all, the Art Loss Register (ALR), the world's largest data bank of lost and stolen artworks, now has more than 300,000 entries!

Besides sensational museum robberies, there are other forms of art theft. To answer the question as to the biggest art robbery of all time, we would probably have to go back two centuries, to Napoleon Bonaparte. On his many campaigns through Europe and North Africa, Napoleon and his army took possession of countless art treasures, including Egyptian grave goods, Greco-Roman sculptures, costly textiles and books—indeed, whole libraries. Napoleon organized his art thefts as carefully as his military exploits. A great many objects of art have never been returned. They are still on view in the Louvre today.

What is art?

“People make art to show what they feel. — People make art to show what they think. — People make art to show how they see the world. — Some people have to make art to be understood. — Some people can only be understood through their art.”

Dietrich von Frank, Art Insurer, Nationale Suisse, Basel

Dietrich von Frank viewing Roman Signer’s sculpture *Rocket III,* 1981, from the collection of Nationale Suisse, Basel

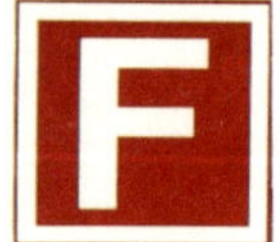

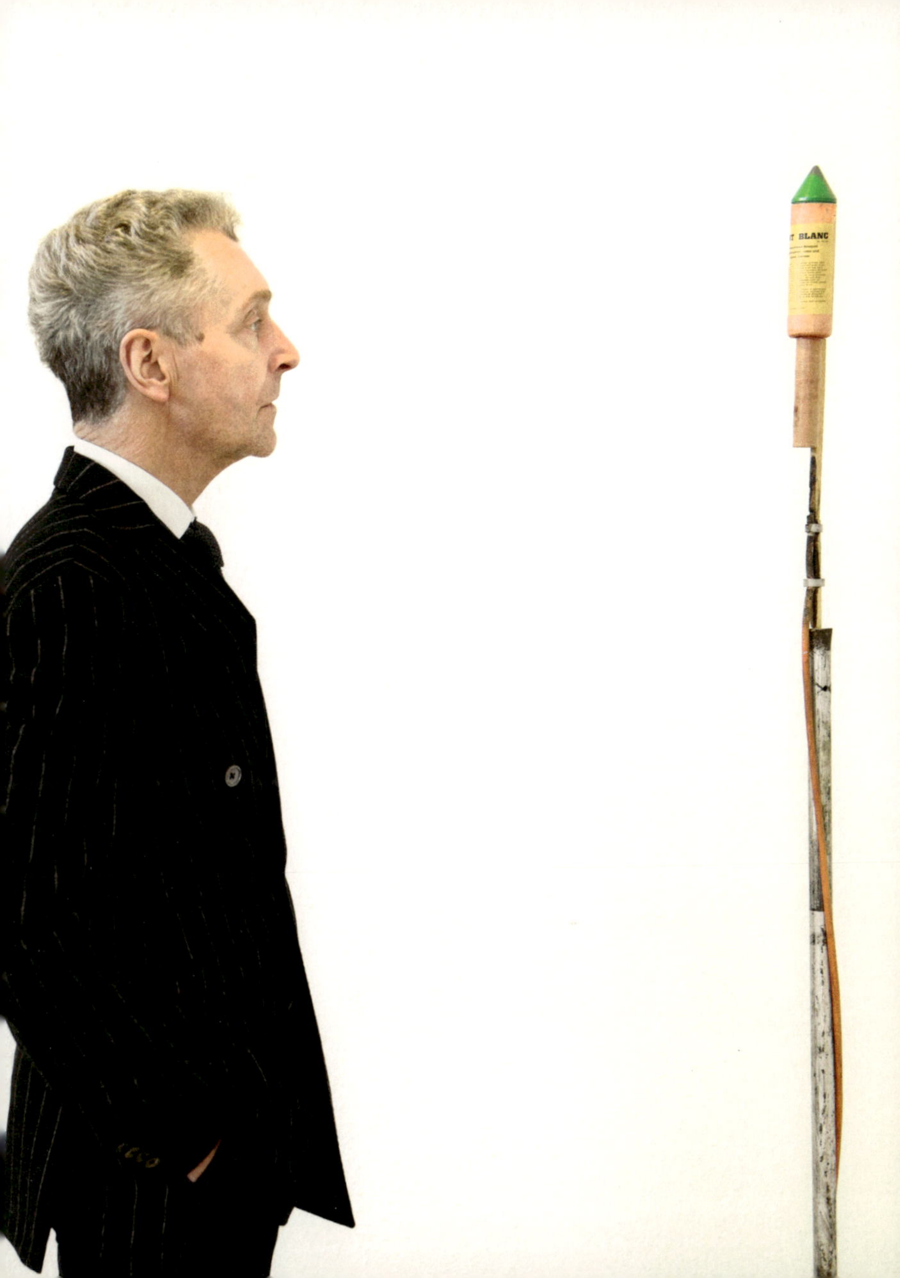
BLANC

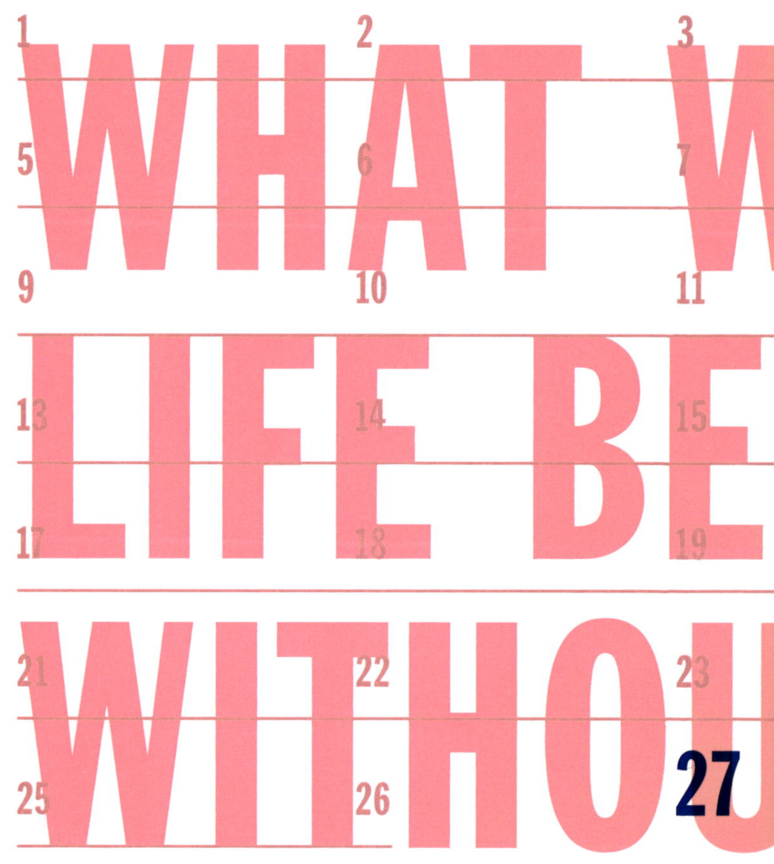
WHAT W
LIFE BE
WITHOU
1
2
3
5
6
7
9
10
11
13
14
15
17
18
19
21
22
23
25
26
27

OULD
LIKE
ART?

27 WHAT WOULD LIFE BE LIKE WITHOUT ART?

This question is difficult to answer. Maybe life without art would look something like this:

There would be noises and lots of tones, but no music.
There would be letters and words, but no stories or poems.
There would be moving pictures, but no good film.
There would be colors and accumulations of dots and lines, but no drawings or paintings.
There would be lots of materials and forms, but no sculpture.

In other words, no special value would be placed on expressing human dreams and ideas.

Without art, literature, and music, people would lack a language to give adequate expression to their feelings, memories, and thoughts. We would never have seen or heard all the invaluable works of the past, and people would know less about themselves and others.

What's difficult to achieve in many areas of life—happiness and perfection—is made possible through art. Time and again. If not for everyone at the same time, at least for individuals and groups of people.

What is art?

"In my view, it's the task of art to define art; it's precisely the lack of a definition that characterizes it. I myself am not an artist, and leave it up to those who are artists to talk about this. On the other hand, I do know what I consider the qualities of art, and what it contributes to society. Art enables the individual to form an opinion about the world. It creates a liberated space where questions can be raised that have no place anywhere else. Art is a field of experimentation beyond compare for new ideas; it's a synonym for renewal and exchange. And, finally, let's not forget that art is a source of enjoyment for people, permitting them to realize themselves and to relax. Without art, there would be no humanity, no civilization, no common life."

Alain Berset, Federal Councillor, Swiss Federal Department of Home Affairs, Bern

Alain Berset at the opening of the 65th Festival del Film Locarno

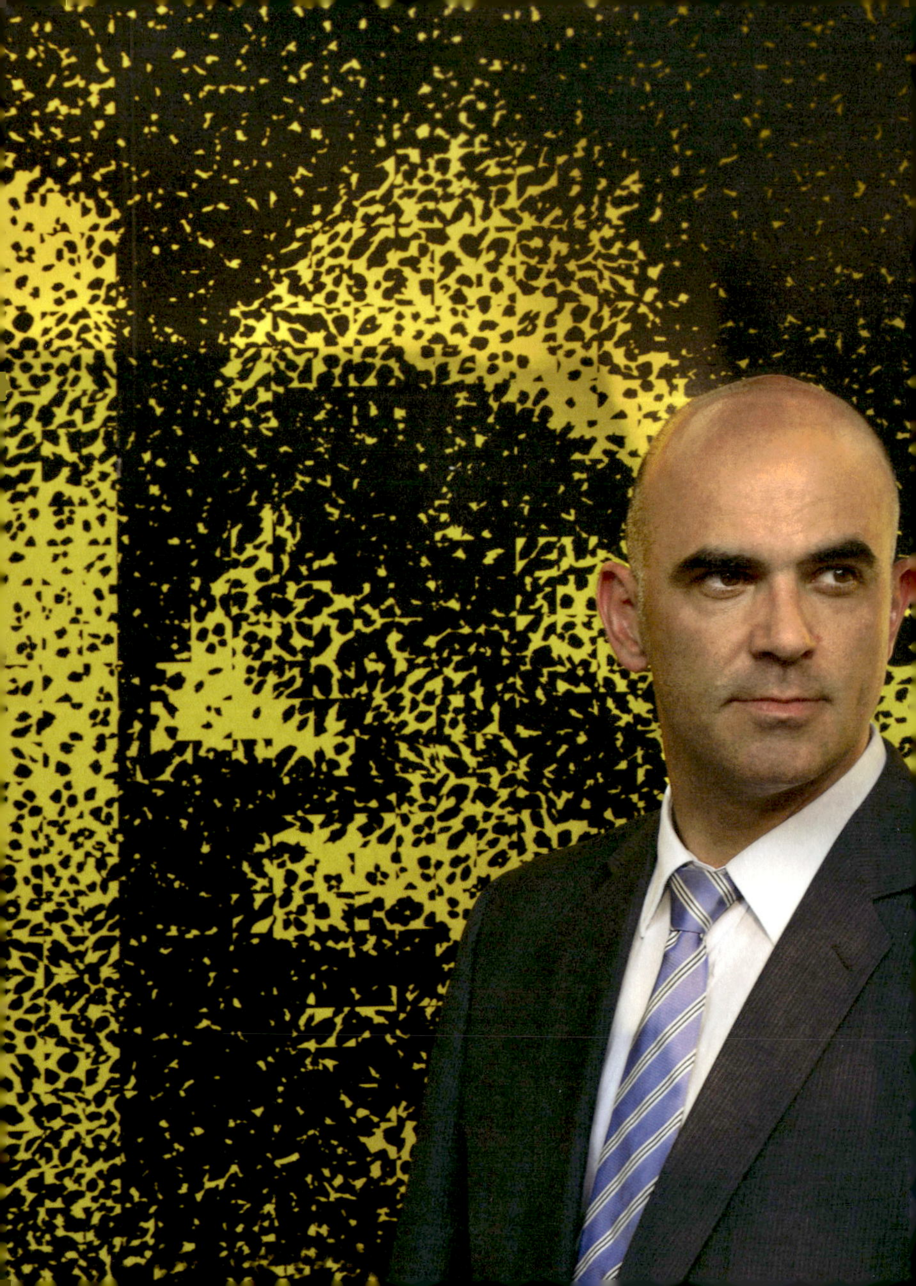

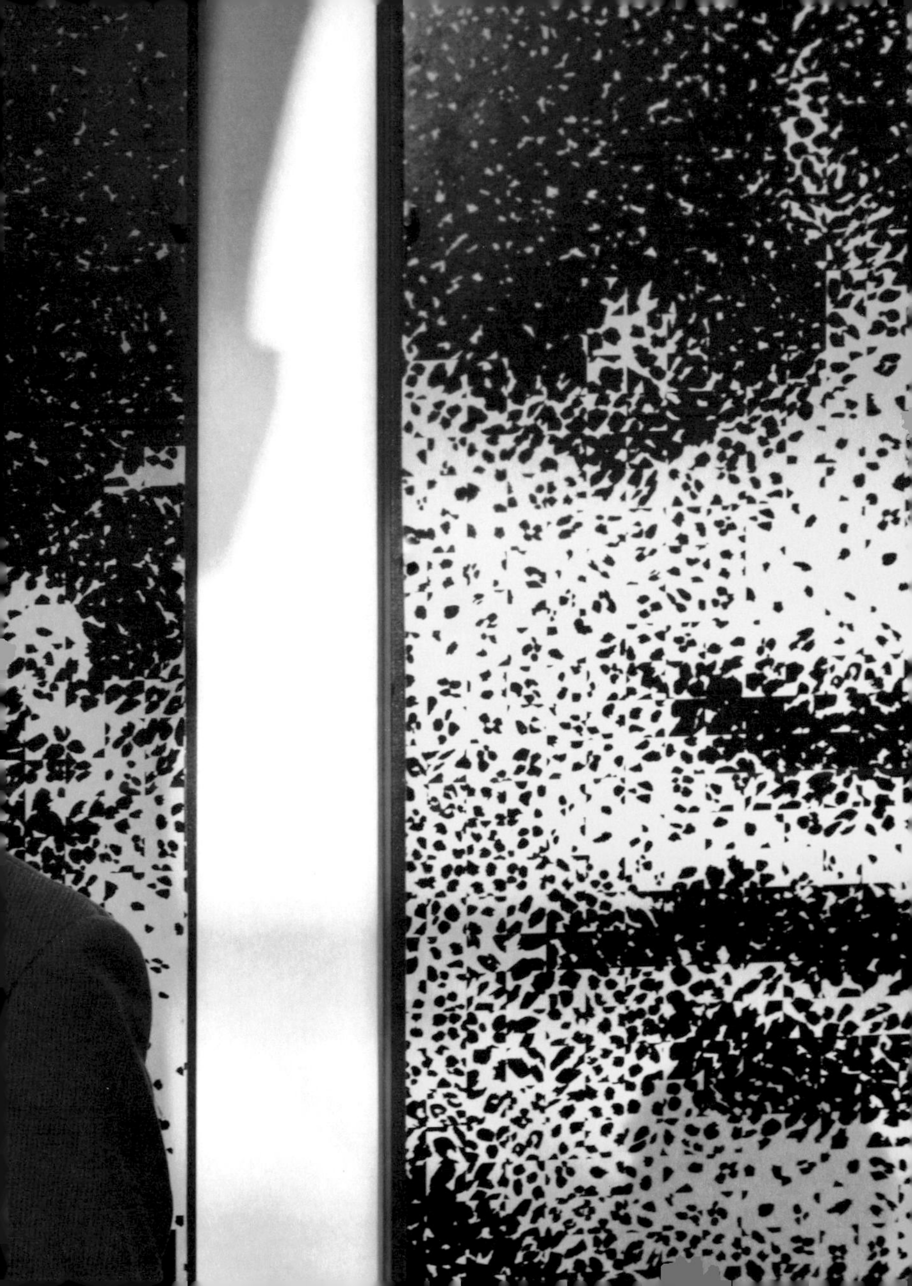

"What is Art?" — A Project of the Fondation Beyeler's Department of Art Education

Twenty-seven questions posed by young people—all earnest, provocative, amusing, and fundamental—are the starting point of our publication *What is Art?*. By answering these questions, this book aims to make art more accessible to adolescents and adults.

Art is something we are confronted with in a wide variety of contexts: not only in museums but also in public spaces, books, magazines, and on the Internet. Art comes in many shapes and colors. It's often not easy to understand what a work of art is, or what point it makes, if any. And when we ask what, in fact, art is, hardly anyone seems capable of giving a clear answer. So why should we waste our precious time standing in front of a work of art and looking at it? Because art is an adventure for the eye. And not only for the eye! Art tells us many interesting things about who we are, how others see the world, and what links us as human beings. Like listening to music, reading books, and watching movies, looking at art is a form of communication.

What's special about this book is that it came about directly through a cooperation with young people. In the course of several workshops, students collected questions about art to which they had always wanted to know the answers. From more than a hundred questions, they eventually selected twenty-seven that they thought most interesting. These were answered by our team of art educators, who have gathered a great deal of experience in working with adolescents at the most frequently visited art museum in Switzerland, the Fondation Beyeler in Riehen/Basel. We also put the fundamental question"What is art?" to well-known Swiss experts in the field. Their statements add up to a patchwork of personal opinions from various points of view. The photographer Andri Pol has portrayed the people involved in their private or professional surroundings and provided images of further sites and situations connected with the appreciation of art.

Conceived and produced by the Fondation Beyeler, this book was designed by Müller+Hess. The UBS not only provided generous support for this project but, as a Partner for Art Education for Families and Young People, has also helped further its distribution.

We wish to thank everyone who contributed to this publication and hope that it is not only fun to read, but also sparks readers' interest in the world of art.

The Artists

Visitors in front of Kezban Arca Batibeki's painting *Light Blue 2*, from the *Pulp Fiction* series, 2010, at the Leila Heller Gallery booth, Art Dubai, 2011

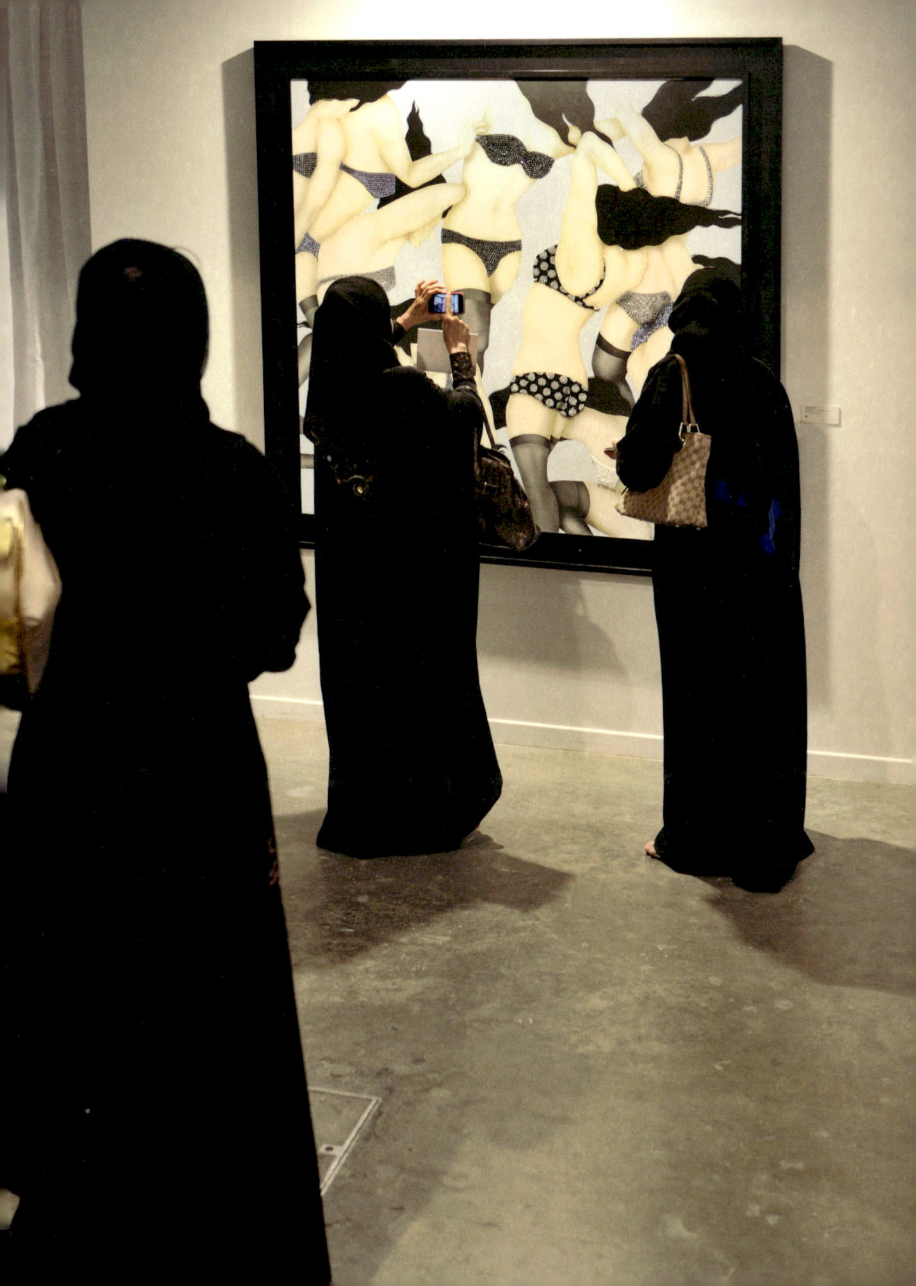

The Experts

The Authors

Stefanie Bringezu (*1977) studied Visual Arts and English Literature in teachers' education at the Universität der Künste and the Freie Universität in Berlin, as well as at the University of the West of England, Bristol. Active as a teacher and art educator. Since 2011, a member of the Fondation Beyeler's Department of Art Education.

Daniel Kramer (*1958) studied German Literature and Art History at the University of Bern. Active since 1998 in the Fondation Beyeler's Department of Art Education. Coauthor of the publication series *ANSICHTEN,* devoted to major works of the Fondation Beyeler.

Janine Schmutz (*1975) studied Art History and History at the Universities of Basel and Freiburg im Breisgau. In 2003–04, scholarly assistant at the Künstlerhaus Schloss Balmoral, Bad Ems, Germany. Since 2004, a member of the Fondation Beyeler's Department of Art Education, of which she became head in 2011. Active at the same time as a freelance curator, writer, and publisher.

The Photographer

Andri Pol (*1961) trained as a drawing instructor at the School of Design, Lucerne; studied photography at the Royal College of Art, London. Since then, active as a freelance portrait photographer and photojournalist for international magazines, and has published numerous books. His work has been honored by many awards.

Acknowledgments

We are extremely grateful to the five school classes that contributed to the preparation of this publication. These young people not only posed many questions about art but gave us valuable tips concerning the clarity and readability of the texts.

Laufental-Thierstein High School, Laufen:
Class 3Z (students majoring in Visual Arts) — Leah Borer, Philomina Chakkalakkal, Lucie Fürst, Salome Jermann, Miriam Kuoni, Gina Labhart
Class 1ILZ — Jasmin Arnold, Corina Borer, Kaitan Borer, Sarah Christ, Vivienne Eggenschwiler, Alina Flückiger, Sabrina Fringeli, Saskia Keller, Chantal Mathys, Xiomara Moron, Leila Müller, Sandra Pfeiffer, Nadine Schneider, Nina Schneider, Lukas Steiner, Sophie Tobler, Manuela Ugolini
Class P4m — Elias Aebi, Luca Bronca, Samuel Cueni, Ramona Dalla Vecchia, Stefanie Dobler, Gracia Fässler, Rachid Freudemann, Laura Gebhardt, Serafin Gerber, Milena Hänggi, Nina Hellinger, Carmen Henz, Valérie Huber, Isabelle Imhof, Valérie Jermann, Tobias Kipfer, Daniel Leupold, Samuel Meury, Sannie Schnell, Dario Thürkauf, Benjamin Troxler
Class 2ABS-IL — Christin Berger, Hannah Gasser, Tobias Glatz, Jasmin Grolimund, Jana Huber, David Huwiler, Benedict Leupold, Michel Lüthi, Victor Misev, Robin Mona, Sven Niederberger, Tamara Rappo, Mithula Satkunam, Katrin Schneider, Anita Schnider, Daniel Volonté, Joshua Wyss

Young people looking into Tala Madani's installation *Loophole,* 2010, at the Pilar Corrias booth, Frieze Art Fair, London, 2010

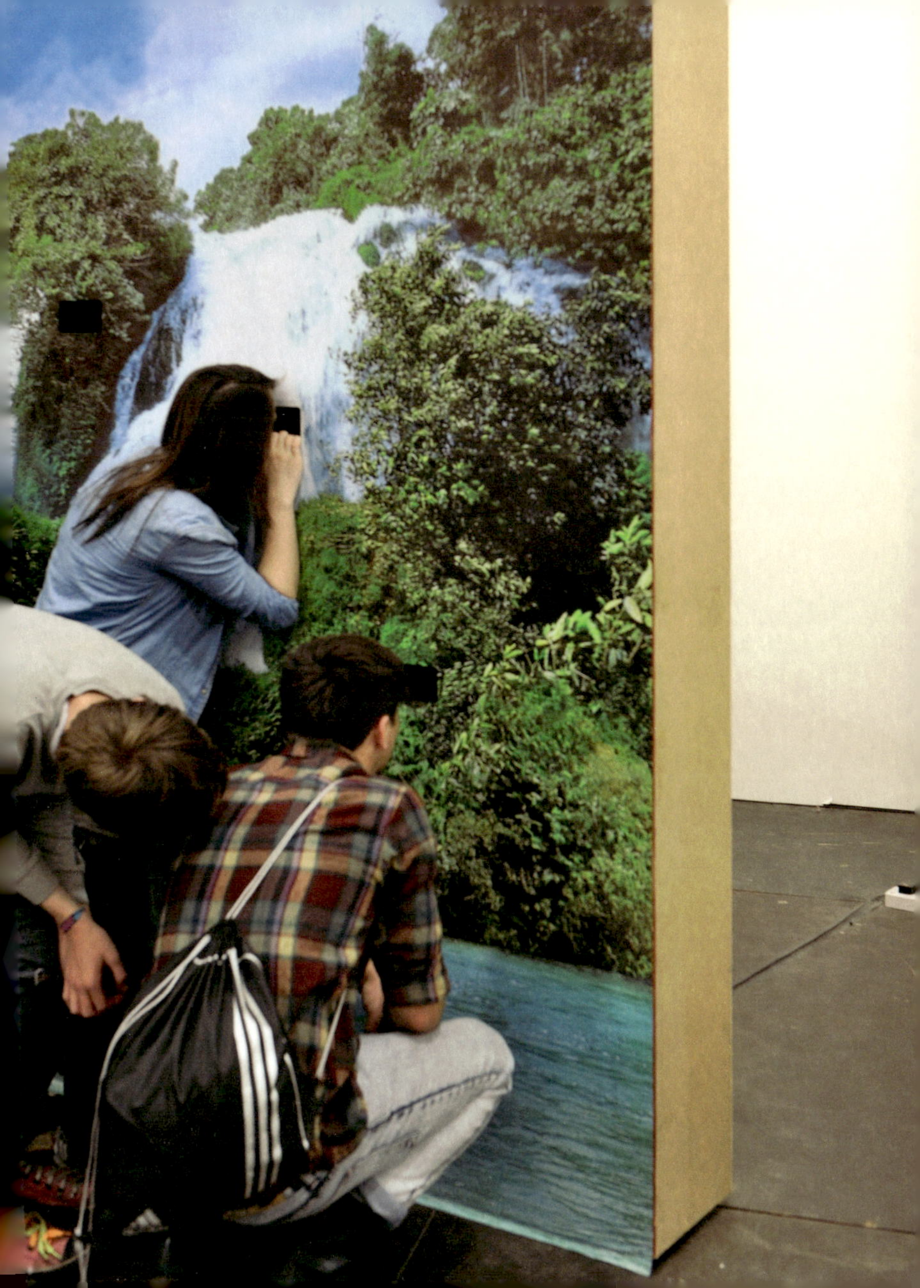

Leonhard High School, Basel:
Class 2e (students majoring in Visual Arts)
Edona Ademaj, Cedric Altermatt, Riane Baur, Marina Bralic, Rachela Castanheira, Stella Elliott, Gerome Gadient, Anna Goetschel, Franz Hagmann, Mattia Hagmann, Gwennaëlle Heini, Miloš Jovanović, Max Keller, Marie-Sophie Kusch, Ines Ljajic, Dario Meister, Anja Mesmer, Alessia Rivolta, Lara Schacher, Linda Schnetzler, Melina Toffol, Lotta Torhorst, Marilène Zipperer

We also wish to express our appreciation to
Michael Baumgartner, Ulrike Berger, Delia Ciuha, Heidi Colsman-Freyberger, John W. Faulkner, Katrin Hager, Kilian Jost, Pia Kuchenmüller, Thomas Lachenmeier, Martin Meury, Werner von Mutzenbecher, Marcel Scheible, Oliver Wick, Denise Zeller, Riccarda Züllig.

List of Illustrations

42–43 — Two children in front of Jeff Koons's sculpture *Naked,* 1988, at the Fondation Beyeler, Riehen/Basel, during the *Jeff Koons* exhibition, 2012.
46–47 — Leah Borer, Lucie Fürst, Gina Labhart, Salome Jermann, Miriam Kuoni, and Philomina Chakkalakkal (from back to front) in Richard Serra's sculpture *Intersection,* 1992, on Theaterplatz in Basel, 2012.
54–55 — Maja Hoffmann next to Olafur Eliasson's *Berlin colour sphere,* 2006, in her London residence, 2012.
62–63 — Hanspeter Marty inspecting Ferdinand Hodler's first version of the painting *Truth,* 1902, Kunsthaus Zürich, 2012.
68–69 — Visitor in front of Pablo Picasso's sculpture *Woman with Hat,* 1961/63, Fondation Beyeler, Riehen/Basel, 2012.
76–77 — Iwan Wirth with Mary Heilmann's works *Rietveld-Remix #3,* 2012, and *Good Vibrations Diptych, Remembering David,* 1992–2011, in the London branch of Hauser & Wirth, 2012, courtesy of Mary Heilmann and Hauser & Wirth.
84–85 — Margrit Hahnloser among works from her collection: Jasper Johns's *Passage I – Working Proof,* 1966 (front); Xerxes Ach's *Painting,* 2008 (back left); Donald Baechler's *Inexplicable Gift,* 2003 (back right); and Tim Scott's *From Matisse II,* 1981; Zurich, 2012.
90–91 — Security guard and Andy Warhol's *Large Campbell's Soup Can,* 1964, in the conference room of Campbell Soup Company, Camden, New Jersey, 2012.
96–97 — Visitor in Sergio Prego's installation *Ikurriña Quarter,* 2010, at the booth of the Galería Soledad Lorenzo at *Art Unlimited,* Art 41 Basel, 2010, courtesy of Sergio Prego and the Galería Soledad Lorenzo.
104–05 — Simon de Pury next to Tim Noble & Sue Webster's *Puny Undernourished Kid* and *Girlfriend from Hell* (diptych), both 2004, in the New York auction rooms of Phillips de Pury & Company, 2012.
110–11 — Young man in front of Henri Rousseau's *The Hungry Lion Attacking an Antilope,* 1898/1905, Fondation Beyeler, Riehen/Basel, 2010.
114–15 — Claudia Blümle viewing slides at the Kunstakademie Münster, 2012.
122–23 — Bice Curiger behind Rebecca Warner's sculpture *Dark Passage,* 2004, Kunsthaus Zürich, 2012.
128–29 — Sam Keller with Jeff Koons's sculpture *Tulips,* 1995–98, Fondation Beyeler, Riehen/Basel, during the *Jeff Koons* exhibition, 2012.
134–35 — Ai Weiwei holding part of his 167-piece sculpture *Mei Le* and standing next to two casts of his sculpture *Marble Arm,* both 2007, in his Beijing studio, February 2007.

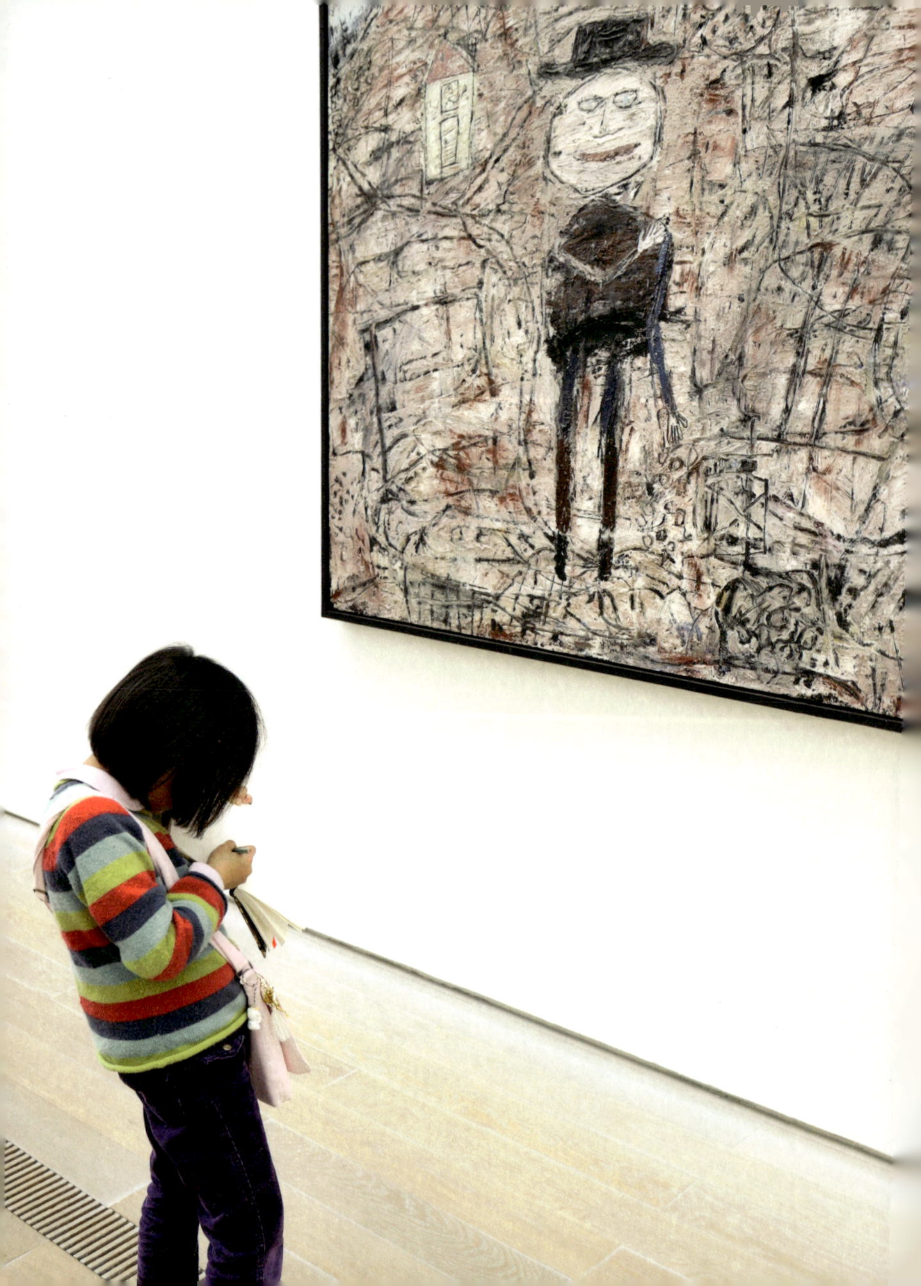

142–43 — Monica Studer and Christoph van den Berg with their installation *A Band of Floating Mushrooms,* 2011, Kunstfreilager Dreispitz, Basel, 2012.
148–49 — Visitors next to David Shrigley's installation *I'm Dead,* 2010, at the Stephen Friedman Gallery booth, Frieze Art Fair, London, 2010.
156–57 — Elodie Pong in her video projection *Ersatz,* 2011, in her Zurich studio, 2012.
162–63 — Visitors in front of Kehinde Wiley's painting *Femme Piquée Par Un Serpent,* 2008, at the Sean Kelly Gallery booth, Art Basel Miami Beach, 2010.
170–71 — Claudia Steinfels in the stairwell of the UBS "Felsenhof" office building in Zurich, 2012.
178–79 — Bertalan Bozsanyi in front of the tapestry *The Shepherd's Life,* early sixteenth century, Oskar Reinhart Collection "Am Römerholz," Winterthur, 2012.
186–87 — John Armleder in the midst of his books in one of his art depots in Geneva, 2012.
194–95 — Dietrich von Frank viewing Roman Signer's sculpture *Rocket III,* 1981, from the collection of Nationale Suisse, Basel, 2012.
200–01 — Alain Berset at the opening of the 65th Festival del Film Locarno, 2012.
207 — Visitors in front of Kezban Arca Batibeki's painting *Light Blue 2,* from the *Pulp Fiction* series, 2010, at the Leila Heller Gallery booth, Art Dubai, 2011, courtesy of the Leila Heller Gallery.
211 — Young people looking into Tala Madani's installation *Loophole,* 2010, at the Pilar Corrias booth, Frieze Art Fair, London, 2010.
214 — Child sketching in front of Jean Dubuffet's *The Lost Traveller,* 1950 (detail), Fondation Beyeler, Riehen/Basel, 2010.
Inside back cover — Visitor in front of Mark Rothko's *Untitled (Red, Orange),* 1968, Fondation Beyeler, Riehen/Basel, 2010. — Young man viewing Jeff Koons's sculptures *Pink Panther* and *Michael Jackson and Bubbles,* both 1988, at the Fondation Beyeler, Riehen/Basel, during the Jeff Koons exhibition, 2012.

Child sketching in front of Jean Dubuffet's *The Lost Traveller,* 1950 (detail), Fondation Beyeler, Riehen/Basel

Colophon

What is Art? 27 Questions, 27 Answers
Issued by the Beyeler Museum AG
Concept: Stefanie Bringezu, Daniel Kramer, Janine Schmutz in collaboration with Müller+Hess
Editing: Valentina Locatelli
Translations from the German: John W. Gabriel
Copyediting: Michele Tilgner
Photographs: Andri Pol
Image processing: Fotofachlabor Pascale Brügger, Julien Contant
Design: Müller+Hess, Beat Müller, Wendelin Hess, Sheena Czorniczek
Typeface: Franklin Gothic, Trade Gothic
Paper: GardaPat Kiara, 135 g/m²
Printing: Gremper AG, Basel/Pratteln
Binding: Buchbinderei Schumacher AG, Schmitten

A publication of the Beyeler Museum AG
Baselstrasse 101
4125 Riehen/Basel, Switzerland
Tel. +41 61 6459700
Fax +41 61 6459719
www.fondationbeyeler.ch
info@fondationbeyeler.ch

ISBN 000-3-905632-99-3 (English)
ISBN 000-3-905632-96-9 (German)
ISBN 000-3-905632-97-7 (French)
ISBN 000-3-905632-98-5 (Italian, available exclusively in the Fondation Beyeler's Art Shop)

The trade edition is published by
Hatje Cantz Verlag
Zeppelinstrasse 32
73760 Ostfildern, Germany
Tel. +49 711 4405200
Fax +49 711 4405220
www.hatjecantz.de

ISBN 978-3-7757-3527-8 (English)
ISBN 978-3-7757-3526-1 (German)
ISBN 978-3-7757-3528-5 (French)

Hatje Cantz books are available internationally at selected bookstores. For more information about our distribution partners, please visit our homepage at www.hatjecantz.com

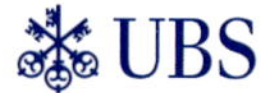

UBS – Partner for Art Education for Families and Young People

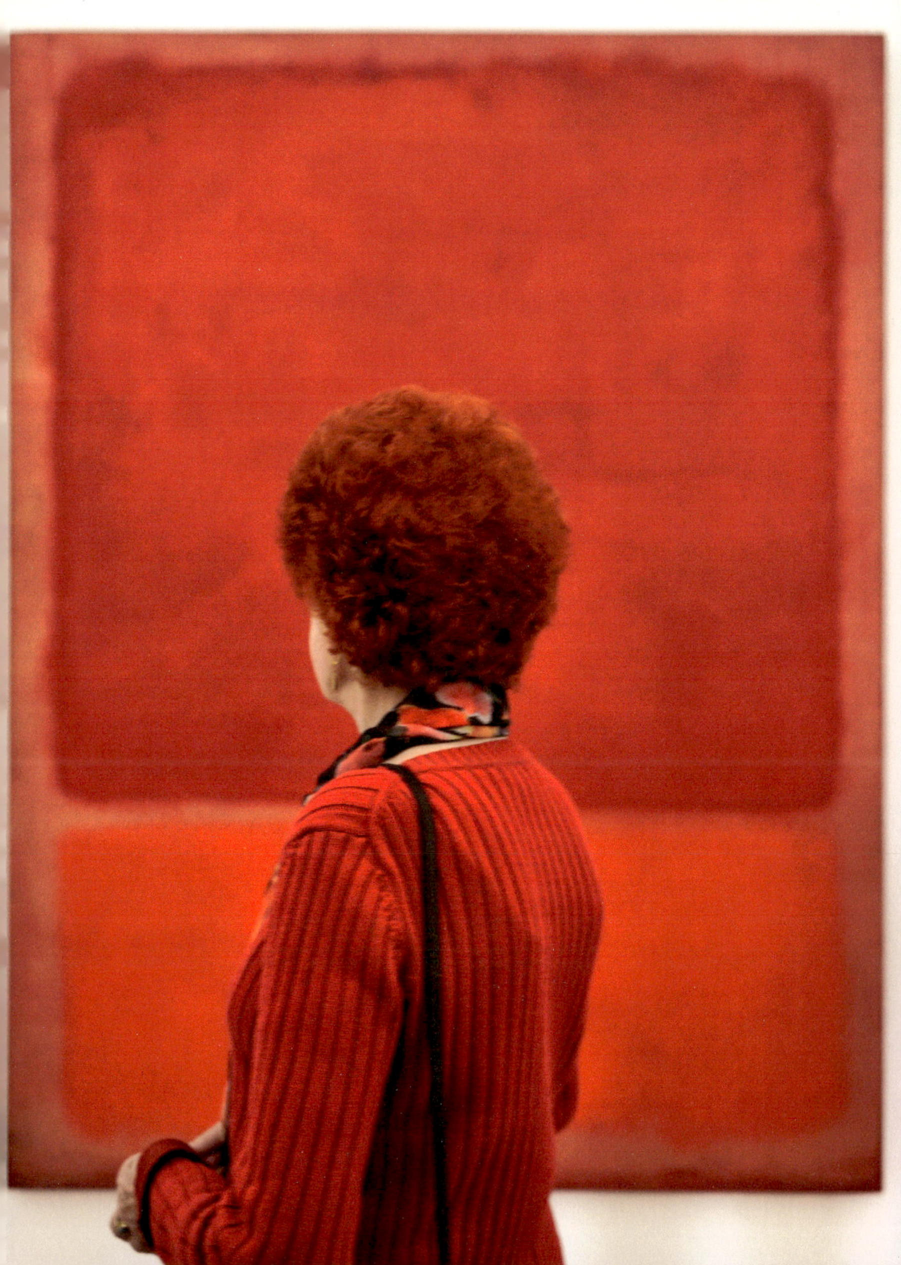

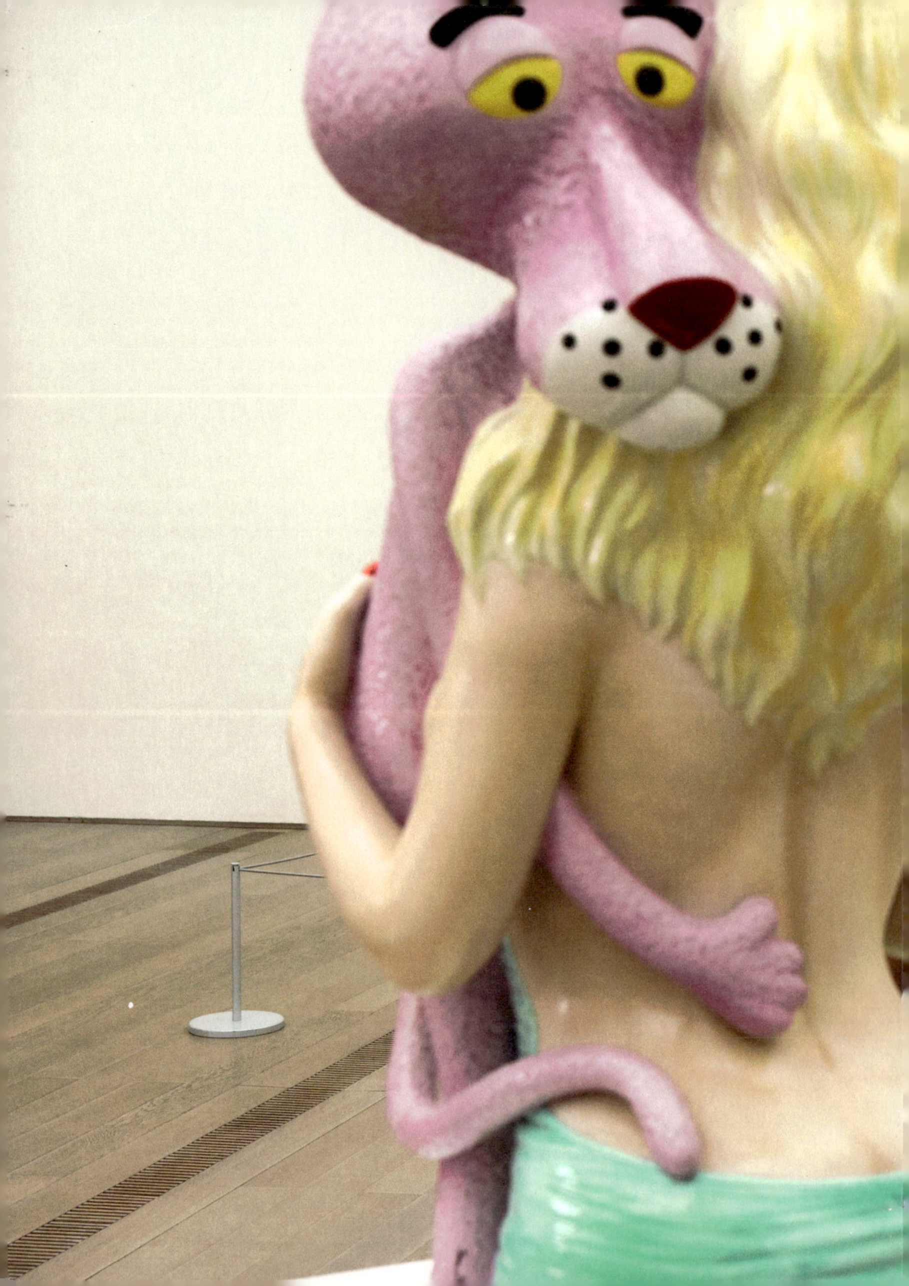